FAVORITE BRAND NAME™

Low-Carb
Recipes

Publications International, Ltd.
Favorite Brand Name Recipes at www.fbnr.com

Pictured on the front cover: Roast Chicken with Peppers *(page 140).*

Pictured on the back cover: Today's Slim Tuna Stuffed Tomatoes *(page 64).*

Inset on the back cover: Low Fat Lemon Soufflé Cheesecake *(page 184).*

ISBN: 0-7853-8053-1

Library of Congress Control Number: 2002112007

Manufactured in China.

8 7 6 5 4 3 2 1

Nutritional Analysis: The nutritional information that appears with each recipe was submitted in part by the participating companies and associations. Every effort has been made to check the accuracy of these numbers. However, because numerous variables account for a wide range of values for certain foods, nutritive analyses in this book should be considered approximate.

Microwave Cooking: Microwave ovens vary in wattage. Use the cooking times as guidelines and check for doneness before adding more time.

Preparation/Cooking Times: Preparation times are based on the approximate amount of time required to assemble the recipe before cooking, baking, chilling or serving. These times include preparation steps such as measuring, chopping and mixing. The fact that some preparations and cooking can be done simultaneously is taken into account. Preparation of optional ingredients and serving suggestions is not included.

Contents

Sweet-Sour Turnip Green Salad

    2 cups shredded stemmed washed turnip greens
    2 cups washed mixed salad greens
    1 cup sliced plum tomatoes or quartered cherry tomatoes
    ½ cup shredded carrot
    ⅓ cup sliced green onions
    8 tablespoons water, divided
    2 teaspoons all-purpose flour
    1 tablespoon packed brown sugar
    ½ teaspoon celery seeds
      Dash pepper
    1 tablespoon white wine vinegar

Combine turnip greens, salad greens, tomatoes and carrot in salad bowl; set aside. Combine green onions and 2 tablespoons water in small saucepan. Bring to a boil over high heat. Reduce heat to medium. Cook, covered, 2 to 3 minutes or until onions are tender.

Mix remaining 6 tablespoons water and flour in small bowl until smooth. Stir into green onions in saucepan. Add brown sugar, celery seeds and pepper; cook and stir until mixture boils and thickens. Cook and stir 1 minute more. Stir in vinegar. Pour hot dressing over salad; toss to coat. Serve immediately.   **Makes 4 servings**

Nutrients per Serving: 49 Calories (7% of calories from fat), <1g Total Fat, <1g Saturated Fat, 0mg Cholesterol, 41mg Sodium, 2g Protein, 11g Carbohydrate, 3g Dietary Fiber

Sweet-Sour Turnip Green Salad

Quick Vegetable & Pesto Salad

¼ cup reduced-fat mayonnaise
¼ cup refrigerated pesto sauce
1 tablespoon balsamic vinegar
6 cups assorted vegetables from salad bar, such as sliced mushrooms,
  shredded carrots, red onion strips, sliced radishes, peas, broccoli florets
  and bell pepper strips (about 1½ pounds)
  Lettuce leaves

1. Combine mayonnaise, pesto and vinegar in large bowl; stir until well blended.

2. Add vegetables; toss well to coat. Cover and refrigerate 10 minutes. Arrange lettuce leaves on salad plates. Top with vegetable mixture. **Makes 6 (1-cup) servings**

Cook's Note: Chill for 30 minutes to improve the flavor of this easy side-dish salad.

Prep time: 15 minutes

Nutrients per Serving: 132 Calories (56% of calories from fat),
9g Total Fat, 2g Saturated Fat, 5mg Cholesterol, 126mg Sodium,
4g Protein, 12g Carbohydrate, 3g Dietary Fiber

Quick Vegetable & Pesto Salad

Hearty Healthy Chicken Salad

1 broiler-fryer chicken, cooked, skinned, boned and cut into chunks
1 cup small macaroni, cooked and drained
3 tomatoes, cubed
1 cup sliced celery
½ cup chopped red bell pepper
3 tablespoons chopped green onions
1 teaspoon salt
½ teaspoon black pepper
¼ teaspoon dried oregano leaves, crushed
1 cup low sodium chicken broth
1 clove garlic, minced
¼ cup white wine vinegar

Combine chicken, macaroni, tomatoes, celery, bell pepper and onions in large bowl. Sprinkle with salt, black pepper and oregano. Place chicken broth and garlic in small saucepan. Bring to a boil over high heat for 10 minutes or until broth is reduced to ½ cup. Add wine vinegar. Pour over salad; mix well. Refrigerate until cold.

Makes 6 servings

Favorite recipe from **National Chicken Council**

Nutrients per Serving: 266 Calories (30% of calories from fat), 9g Total Fat, 2g Saturated Fat, 101mg Cholesterol, 482mg Sodium, 35g Protein, 11g Carbohydrate, 2g Dietary Fiber

Hearty Healthy Chicken Salad

Fresh Greens
with Hot Bacon Dressing

3 cups torn spinach leaves
3 cups torn romaine lettuce
2 small tomatoes, cut into wedges
1 cup sliced mushrooms
1 medium carrot, shredded
1 slice bacon, cut into small pieces
3 tablespoons red wine vinegar
1 tablespoon water
¼ teaspoon dried tarragon, crushed
⅛ teaspoon coarsely ground pepper
¼ teaspoon EQUAL® FOR RECIPES *or* 1 packet EQUAL® sweetener *or*
    2 teaspoons EQUAL® SPOONFUL™

• Combine spinach, romaine, tomatoes, mushrooms and carrot in large bowl; set aside.

• Cook bacon in 12-inch skillet until crisp. Carefully stir in vinegar, water, tarragon and pepper. Heat to boiling; remove from heat. Stir in Equal.®

• Add spinach mixture to skillet. Toss 30 to 60 seconds or just until greens are wilted. Transfer to serving bowl. Serve immediately.   **Makes 4 to 6 (1⅓-cup) servings**

Nutrients per Serving: 51 Calories (17% of calories from fat),
1g Total Fat, <1g Saturated Fat, 1mg Cholesterol, 74mg Sodium,
4g Protein, 8g Carbohydrate, 3g Dietary Fiber

Fresh Greens with Hot Bacon Dressing

Santa Fe Grilled Vegetable Salad

- 2 baby eggplants (6 ounces each), halved
- 1 medium yellow summer squash, halved
- 1 medium zucchini, halved
- 1 green bell pepper, cored and quartered
- 1 red bell pepper, cored and quartered
- 1 small onion, peeled and halved
- ½ cup orange juice
- 2 tablespoons lime juice
- 1 tablespoon olive oil
- 2 cloves garlic, minced
- 1 teaspoon dry oregano leaves
- ¼ teaspoon black pepper
- ¼ teaspoon ground red pepper
- ¼ teaspoon salt
- 2 tablespoons chopped fresh cilantro

1. Combine all ingredients except cilantro in large bowl; toss to coat.

2. To prevent sticking, spray grid with nonstick cooking spray. Prepare coals for direct grilling. Place vegetables on grill, 2 to 3 inches from hot coals; reserve marinade. Grill 3 to 4 minutes per side or until tender and lightly charred; cool 10 minutes. Or, place vegetables on rack of broiler pan coated with nonstick cooking spray; reserve marinade. Broil 2 to 3 inches from heat, 3 to 4 minutes per side or until tender; cool 10 minutes.

3. Remove peel from eggplant, if desired. Slice vegetables into bite-size pieces; return to marinade. Stir in cilantro; toss to coat.   **Makes 8 servings**

Nutrients per Serving: 63 Calories (27% of calories from fat), 2g Total Fat, <1g Saturated Fat, <1mg Cholesterol, 70mg Sodium, 2g Protein, 11g Carbohydrate, 1g Dietary Fiber

Santa Fe Grilled Vegetable Salad

Gazpacho Salad

1 cup diced tomato
½ cup diced peeled cucumber
¼ cup diced green pepper
2 tablespoons diced red pepper
2 tablespoons thinly sliced green onion
2 tablespoons vinegar
¼ teaspoon pepper
⅛ teaspoon garlic powder (optional)
1½ cups tomato juice
1 package (4-serving size) JELL-O® Brand Lemon Flavor Sugar Free Low Calorie Gelatin Dessert or JELL-O® Brand Lemon Flavor Gelatin Dessert
Crackers (optional)

MIX vegetables, vinegar, pepper and garlic powder in medium bowl; set aside. Bring tomato juice to boil in small saucepan. Stir into gelatin in large bowl at least 2 minutes until completely dissolved. Refrigerate about 1¼ hours or until slightly thickened (consistency of unbeaten egg whites).

STIR in vegetable mixture. Pour into 4-cup mold.

REFRIGERATE 3 hours or until firm. Unmold. Serve with crackers if desired. Garnish as desired.

Makes 6 servings

Preparation Time: 20 minutes
Refrigerating Time: 4¼ hours

Nutrients per Serving (using JELL-O® Brand Lemon Flavor Sugar Free Low Calorie Gelatin Dessert): 28 Calories (5% of calories from fat), <1g Total Fat, <1g Saturated Fat, 0mg Cholesterol, 260mg Sodium, 2g Protein, 5g Carbohydrate, <1g Dietary Fiber

FREE PREVIEW ISSUE

Yes! Send my FREE preview issue of LOW-CARB LIFESTYLE Magazine today and start my subscription. If I like what I see, I'll get three more issues for only $9.95—that's a 38% savings off the cover price! If I'm not delighted, I'll just write "cancel" on the invoice and owe nothing. I'll keep the FREE issue no matter what.

Name

Address

City/State/ZIP

No risk. No obligation.
Just mail this card today!

S69DGA

Every recipe **15**g carbs or less per serving

All-New
LOW-CARB
Lifestyle

Recipes for breakfasts, sides, **main dishes**, and desserts

**Low-Carb,
High-Flavor Recipes!**

BUSINESS REPLY MAIL

FIRST-CLASS MAIL   PERMIT NO. 24   MT. MORRIS, IL

POSTAGE WILL BE PAID BY ADDRESSEE

LOW-CARB LIFESTYLE
PO BOX 512
MT MORRIS IL 61054-7912

Gazpacho Salad

SPAM® and Peanut Salad

Dressing
- ⅓ cup rice wine vinegar
- ¼ cup CARAPELLI® extra virgin olive oil
- 2 tablespoons peanut butter
- 1 tablespoon HOUSE OF TSANG® Soy Sauce
- 1 teaspoon sugar
- ¼ teaspoon ground ginger
- 1 garlic clove, minced

Salad
- 2 cups shredded napa cabbage or lettuce
- 2 cups shredded romaine lettuce
- 1 (12-ounce) can SPAM® Luncheon Meat, cut into 2-inch strips
- 1 cup shredded carrots
- 1 cup fresh or thawed frozen pea pods
- ½ cup roasted peanuts
- ¼ cup chopped green onions

In small bowl, using wire whisk or fork, whisk together all dressing ingredients. In large bowl, combine all salad ingredients. Drizzle with dressing.   **Makes 6 servings**

Nutrients per Serving: 326 Calories (72% of calories from fat),
26g Total Fat, 8g Saturated Fat, 46mg Cholesterol, 676mg Sodium,
15g Protein, 11g Carbohydrate, 5g Dietary Fiber

Spicy Chayote Carrot Slaw

1 pound peeled chayote, quartered
1 cup grated carrots
¼ cup minced jalapeño peppers
½ cup sour orange juice (*or* ¼ cup fresh orange juice and ¼ cup fresh lime juice)
1 tablespoon olive oil
½ teaspoon minced habanero peppers
1 packet NatraTaste® Brand Sugar Substitute
¼ teaspoon garlic powder
¼ teaspoon salt

1. In a medium saucepan, bring 2 inches of water to a boil. Add chayote, cover and cook for 2 to 3 minutes. Drain, rinse with cold water, and when cool enough to handle, grate to yield about 3 cups. Combine with carrots in a bowl.

2. Combine remaining ingredients in a small jar with a lid. Shake; pour dressing over salad, and toss. Serve immediately or cover and refrigerate. Serve within 1 day for maximum crispness.   **Makes 4 servings**

Nutrients per Serving: 90 Calories (40% of calories from fat), 4g Total Fat, <1g Saturated Fat, 0mg Cholesterol, 220mg Sodium, 2g Protein, 12g Carbohydrate, 3g Dietary Fiber

Three-Pepper Tuna Salad

  2 cups thinly sliced zucchini
  ½ cup red bell pepper strips
  ½ cup green bell pepper strips
  ½ cup yellow bell pepper strips
  1 cup cherry tomatoes, halved
  1 can (6 ounces) solid albacore tuna packed in water, drained and flaked
  ¼ cup chopped green onions with tops
  ¼ cup chopped fresh basil
2½ tablespoons red wine vinegar
  1 tablespoon olive oil
  ½ teaspoon minced fresh garlic
  ½ teaspoon fresh marjoram
  ⅛ teaspoon black pepper

1. Pour ¾ cup water into medium saucepan. Add zucchini and bell pepper strips. Steam vegetables about 10 minutes or until crisp-tender. Remove from heat; drain any excess water. Transfer to serving bowl. Add tomatoes, tuna, green onions and basil.

2. Combine vinegar, oil, garlic, marjoram and black pepper in jar or bottle with tight-fitting lid; shake well. Pour dressing over vegetable mixture; mix well. Garnish as desired.

Makes 4 servings

Nutrients per Serving: 134 Calories (34% of calories from fat), 5g Total Fat, 1g Saturated Fat, 18mg Cholesterol, 175mg Sodium, 14g Protein, 11g Carbohydrate, 3g Dietary Fiber

Three-Pepper Tuna Salad

Grilled Chicken au Poivre Salad

    4 boneless skinless chicken breast halves (about 1¼ pounds)
    ¼ cup plus 3 tablespoons olive oil, divided
    ¼ cup finely chopped onion
    3 cloves garlic, minced
 2½ tablespoons white wine vinegar, divided
    2 teaspoons cracked or coarse ground black pepper
    ½ teaspoon salt
    ¼ teaspoon poultry seasoning
    1 tablespoon Dijon mustard
      Dash sugar
    1 bag (10 ounces) prewashed salad greens
    4 cherry tomatoes, halved

Place chicken, ¼ cup oil, onion, garlic, 1 tablespoon vinegar, pepper, salt, and poultry seasoning in resealable plastic food storage bag. Seal bag; knead to coat chicken. Refrigerate at least 2 hours or overnight.

Grill chicken, on covered grill, over medium-hot coals 10 to 15 minutes or until chicken is no longer pink in center.

For dressing

Combine remaining 3 tablespoons oil, 1½ tablespoons vinegar, mustard and sugar in small bowl; whisk until smooth.

Arrange salad greens and cherry tomatoes on 4 plates.

Cut chicken crosswise into strips. Arrange strips on top of greens. Drizzle with dressing.

Makes 4 servings

Nutrients per Serving: 307 Calories (55% of calories from fat), 17g Total Fat, 2g Saturated Fat, 69mg Cholesterol, 398mg Sodium, 28g Protein, 11g Carbohydrate, 3g Dietary Fiber

Grilled Chicken au Poivre Salad

Melon Salad

2½ cups boiling apple juice

1 package (8-serving size) or 2 packages (4-serving size) JELL-O® Brand Watermelon Flavor Sugar Free Low Calorie Gelatin Dessert or JELL-O® Brand Watermelon Flavor Gelatin Dessert

1½ cups cold seltzer or club soda

1 teaspoon lemon juice

2 cups cantaloupe and honeydew melon cubes

STIR boiling juice into gelatin in large bowl at least 2 minutes until completely dissolved. Stir in cold seltzer and lemon juice. Refrigerate about 1½ hours or until thickened (spoon drawn through leaves definite impression). Stir in melon cubes. Spoon into 6-cup mold.

REFRIGERATE 4 hours or until firm. Unmold. Garnish as desired.

Makes 10 servings

Preparation Time: 15 minutes
Refrigerating Time: 5½ hours

Nutrients per Serving (using JELL-O® Brand Watermelon Flavor Sugar Free Low Calorie Gelatin Dessert and omitting garnish): 50 Calories (0% of calories from fat), 0g Total Fat, 0g Saturated Fat, 0mg Cholesterol, 60mg Sodium, 1g Protein, 10g Carbohydrate, 0g Dietary Fiber

Melon Salad

Red and Green Cabbage Slaw

2½ cups thinly sliced red cabbage
2½ cups thinly sliced green cabbage
 ½ cup chopped yellow or red bell pepper
 ½ cup chopped carrot
 ⅓ cup chopped red onion
 8 ounces reduced-fat Cheddar cheese, cubed
 ½ cup fat-free mayonnaise
 1 tablespoon red wine vinegar
2½ teaspoons EQUAL® FOR RECIPES *or* 8 packets EQUAL® sweetener *or* ⅓ cup
    EQUAL® SPOONFUL™
 ¼ teaspoon celery seed
    Salt and pepper
    Lettuce leaves (optional)

• Combine vegetables and cheese in bowl. Mix mayonnaise, vinegar, Equal® and celery seed; stir into cabbage mixture. Season to taste with salt and pepper.

• Spoon mixture onto lettuce-lined plates, if desired.   **Makes 8 servings**

Tip: Packaged cole slaw vegetables can be used; use 6 cups vegetables and add onion, cheese and mayonnaise dressing as above. Any desired flavor of reduced-fat cheese can be substituted for the Cheddar cheese.

Nutrients per Serving: 83 Calories (22% of calories from fat),
2g Total Fat, 4g Saturated Fat, 6mg Cholesterol, 184mg Sodium,
8g Protein, 9g Carbohydrate, 1g Dietary Fiber

Red and Green Cabbage Slaw

Beef & Blue Cheese Salad

1 package (10 ounces) mixed green lettuce leaves
4 ounces sliced rare deli roast beef, cut into thin strips
1 large tomato, seeded and coarsely chopped *or* 8 large cherry tomatoes,
    halved
2 ounces (½ cup) crumbed blue or Gorgonzola cheese
1 cup croutons
½ cup prepared Caesar or Italian salad dressing

1. In large bowl, combine lettuce, roast beef, tomato, cheese and croutons.

2. Drizzle with dressing; toss well. Serve immediately.

Makes 4 main-dish or 8 side-dish servings

Serving Suggestion: Serve with warm crusty French bread.

Cook's Note: Gorgonzola is one of Italy's great cheeses. It has an ivory-colored interior that is streaked with bluish-green veins. Gorgonzola is made from cow's milk and has a creamy savory flavor. It can be found cut into wedges and wrapped in foil in most supermarkets.

Prep Time: 10 minutes

Nutrients per Serving: 269 Calories (70% of calories from fat),
19g Total Fat, 5g Saturated Fat, 33mg Cholesterol, 528mg Sodium,
11g Protein, 12g Carbohydrate, 2g Dietary Fiber

Beef & Blue Cheese Salad

Hot Chinese Chicken Salad

     8 ounces fresh or steamed Chinese egg noodles
    ¼ cup fat-free, reduced-sodium chicken broth
     2 tablespoons reduced-sodium soy sauce
     2 tablespoons rice wine vinegar
     1 tablespoon rice wine or dry sherry
     1 teaspoon sugar
    ½ teaspoon red pepper flakes
     1 tablespoon vegetable oil, divided
     1 clove garlic, minced
    1½ cups fresh pea pods, sliced diagonally
     1 cup thinly sliced green or red bell pepper
     1 pound boneless skinless chicken breasts, cut into ½-inch pieces
     1 cup thinly sliced red or green cabbage
     2 green onions, thinly sliced

Cook noodles in boiling water 4 to 5 minutes or until tender. Drain; set aside. Blend chicken broth, soy sauce, vinegar, rice wine, sugar and red pepper flakes in small bowl; set aside.

Heat 1 teaspoon oil in large nonstick skillet or wok. Add garlic, pea pods and bell pepper; cook 1 to 2 minutes or until vegetables are crisp-tender. Set aside.

Heat remaining 2 teaspoons oil in skillet. Add chicken; cook 3 to 4 minutes or until chicken is no longer pink. Add cabbage, cooked vegetables and noodles. Stir in sauce; toss until well blended. Cook and stir 1 to 2 minutes or until heated through. Sprinkle with green onions before serving.   **Makes 6 (1⅓-cup) servings**

Nutrients per Serving: 164 Calories (30% of calories from fat), 6g Total Fat, 1g Saturated Fat, 45mg Cholesterol, 353mg Sodium, 17g Protein, 12g Carbohydrate, 2g Dietary Fiber

Hot Chinese Chicken Salad

Cool and Creamy Pea Salad with Cucumbers and Red Onion

2 tablespoons finely chopped red onion
1 tablespoon reduced-fat mayonnaise
⅛ teaspoon salt
⅛ teaspoon black pepper
½ cup frozen green peas, thawed
¼ cup diced red bell pepper
¼ cup diced cucumber

1. Combine onion, mayonnaise, salt and pepper in medium bowl; stir until well blended.

2. Add remaining ingredients and toss gently to coat.   **Makes 2 (½-cup) servings**

Nutrients per Serving: 65 Calories (36% of calories from fat),
3g Total Fat, 1g Saturated Fat, 3mg Cholesterol, 238mg Sodium,
2g Protein, 8g Carbohydrate, 3g Dietary Fiber

Strawberry Banana Salad

1½ cups boiling water
1 package (8-serving size) *or* 2 packages (4-serving size each) JELL-O® Brand
    Strawberry or Strawberry Banana Flavor Sugar Free Low Calorie Gelatin
2 cups cold water
1 cup chopped strawberries
1 banana, sliced

STIR boiling water into gelatin in large bowl at least 2 minutes until completely dissolved. Stir in cold water. Refrigerate about 1½ hours or until thickened (spoon drawn through leaves definite impression).

STIR in strawberries and banana. Pour into 5-cup mold that has been sprayed with no stick cooking spray.

REFRIGERATE 4 hours or until firm. Unmold. Store leftover gelatin mold in refrigerator.
Makes 10 (½-cup) servings

Prep Time: 15 minutes
Refrigerate Time: 5½ hours

Nutrients per Serving: 25 Calories (<1% of calories from fat),
<1g Total Fat, <1g Saturated Fat, 0mg Cholesterol, 50mg Sodium,
1g Protein, 4g Carbohydrate, 1g Dietary Fiber

Marinated Swordfish Salad

2 pounds Florida swordfish fillets*
¼ cup chopped Florida green onions
¼ cup olive oil
3 tablespoons wine vinegar
2 tablespoons capers
3 cloves Florida garlic, minced
2 teaspoons chopped Florida cilantro
½ teaspoon salt
½ teaspoon white pepper
½ teaspoon dried basil
Florida salad greens

*Seafood alternatives: Florida mahi-mahi or shark

Cut fish into 1-inch pieces and broil 5 to 6 inches from heat 3 to 5 minutes or until fish flakes easily. Remove from heat and transfer to cool plate; set aside. Combine remaining ingredients, except salad greens, in large bowl. Mix well and place in flat-bottom container with lid. Place fish in single layer in marinade and close lid tightly; chill 2 hours. Remove fish from marinade and arrange on salad greens.

Makes 6 servings

Favorite recipe from **Florida Department of Agriculture and Consumer Services, Bureau of Seafood and Aquaculture**

Nutrients per Serving: 220 Calories (32% of calories from fat), 10g Total Fat, 2g Saturated Fat, 75mg Cholesterol, 171mg Sodium, 32g Protein, 2g Carbohydrate, <1g Dietary Fiber

Salad Primavera

6 cups romaine lettuce, washed and torn into bite-sized pieces
1 package (9 ounces) frozen artichoke hearts, thawed, drained and cut into
    bite-sized pieces
1 cup chopped watercress
1 orange, peeled and separated into segments and cut into halves
½ cup chopped red bell pepper
¼ cup chopped green onions with tops
    Citrus-Caper Dressing (recipe follows)
2 tablespoons freshly grated Parmesan cheese

Combine lettuce, artichoke hearts, watercress, orange segments, bell pepper and green onions in large bowl. Prepare Citrus-Caper Dressing. Toss dressing with lettuce mixture. Sprinkle with Parmesan before serving.   **Makes 8 servings**

Citrus-Caper Dressing

⅓ cup orange juice
¼ cup white wine vinegar
2 tablespoons chopped fresh parsley
2 teaspoons Dijon mustard
1 tablespoon minced capers
1 teaspoon sugar
1 teaspoon minced garlic
¼ teaspoon black pepper
¼ teaspoon olive oil

Combine all ingredients in jar or bottle with tight-fitting lid; shake well. Refrigerate until ready to serve. Shake well before serving.   **Makes ½ cup dressing**

Nutrients per Serving: 55 Calories (14% of calories from fat),
1g Total Fat, <1g Saturated Fat, 1mg Cholesterol, 102mg Sodium,
3g Protein, 10g Carbohydrate, 3g Dietary Fiber

Salad Primavera

Cobb Salad

1 package (10 ounces) torn mixed salad greens *or* **8 cups torn romaine lettuce**
6 ounces deli chicken, turkey or smoked turkey breast, cut ¼ inch thick
1 large tomato, seeded and chopped
⅓ cup bacon bits or crumbled crisply cooked bacon
1 large ripe avocado, diced
⅓ cup prepared blue cheese or Caesar salad dressing

1. Place lettuce in salad bowl.

2. Dice chicken; place in center of lettuce.

3. Arrange tomato, bacon and avocado in rows on either side of chicken.

4. Add dressing. Serve immediately.　　　　**Makes 4 main-dish or 8 side-dish servings**

Serving suggestion: Serve with warm French or Italian rolls, if desired.

Preparation time: 15 minutes

Nutrients per Serving: 194 Calories (56% of calories from fat),
12g Total Fat, 4g Saturated Fat, 28mg Cholesterol, 957mg Sodium,
13g Protein, 11g Carbohydrate, 4g Dietary Fiber

Cobb Salad

Garden Greens with Fennel Dressing

Dressing
- ½ teaspoon unflavored gelatin
- 2 tablespoons cold water
- ¼ cup boiling water
- ½ teaspoon salt
- ½ teaspoon sugar
- ¼ cup raspberry or wine vinegar
- 1 tablespoon fresh lemon juice
- ¼ teaspoon dry mustard
- ¼ teaspoon anise extract or ground fennel seeds
- ⅛ teaspoon black pepper
- 1¼ teaspoons walnut or canola oil

Salad
- 1 head (10 ounces) Bibb lettuce, washed and torn into bite-sized pieces
- 1 head (10 ounces) radicchio, washed and torn into bite-sized pieces
- 1 bunch arugula (3 ounces), washed and torn into bite-sized pieces
- 1 cup mâche or spinach leaves, washed and torn into bite-sized pieces
- 1 fennel bulb (8 ounces), finely chopped (reserve fern for garnish)
- 1 tablespoon pine nuts, toasted

To prepare dressing, sprinkle gelatin over cold water in small bowl; let stand 1 minute to soften. Add boiling water; stir 2 minutes or until gelatin is completely dissolved. Add salt and sugar; stir until sugar is completely dissolved. Add all remaining dressing ingredients except oil; mix well. Slowly whisk in oil until well blended. Cover and refrigerate 2 hours or overnight. Shake well before using.

To prepare salad, place all salad ingredients except pine nuts in large bowl. Add dressing; toss until all leaves glisten. Divide salad among 6 chilled salad plates. Top each salad with ½ teaspoon pine nuts. Garnish with sprig of fennel fern, if desired.

Makes 6 servings

Nutrients per Serving: 60 Calories (30% of calories from fat), 2g Total Fat, <1g Saturated Fat, 0mg Cholesterol, 226mg Sodium, 3g Protein, 9g Carbohydrate, 1g Dietary Fiber

Garden Greens with Fennel Dressing

Garlic Lovers' Chicken Caesar Salad

DRESSING
 1 can (10¾ ounces) reduced-fat condensed cream of chicken soup
 ½ cup fat-free, low sodium chicken broth
 ¼ cup balsamic vinegar
 ¼ cup fat free shredded Parmesan cheese, divided
 3 cloves garlic, minced
 1 tablespoon low sodium Worcestershire sauce
 ¼ teaspoon black pepper

SALAD
 2 heads romaine lettuce, torn into 2-inch pieces
 4 grilled boneless skinless chicken breast halves, cut into 2-inch strips
 ½ cup fat-free herb-seasoned croutons

Combine soup, chicken broth, vinegar, 2 tablespoons Parmesan cheese, garlic, Worcestershire sauce and pepper in food processor or blender; process until smooth. Combine lettuce and 1 cup dressing in large salad bowl; toss well to coat. Top with chicken and croutons; sprinkle with remaining 2 tablespoons cheese.

Makes 8 servings

Nutrients per Serving: 132 Calories (15% of calories from fat),
2g Total Fat, 1g Saturated Fat, 40mg Cholesterol, 185mg Sodium,
17g Protein, 10g Carbohydrate, 1g Dietary Fiber

Garlic Lovers' Chicken Caesar Salad

Hearty Soups

Spicy Pumpkin Soup with Green Chili Swirl

1 can (4 ounces) diced green chilies
¼ cup reduced-fat sour cream
¼ cup fresh cilantro leaves
1 can (15 ounces) solid-pack pumpkin
1 can (about 14 ounces) fat-free reduced-sodium chicken broth
½ cup water
1 teaspoon ground cumin
½ teaspoon chili powder
¼ teaspoon garlic powder
⅛ teaspoon ground red pepper (optional)
Additional sour cream (optional)

1. Combine green chilies, ¼ cup sour cream and cilantro in food processor or blender; process until smooth.*

2. Combine pumpkin, chicken broth, water, cumin, chili powder, garlic powder and red pepper, if desired, in medium saucepan; stir in ¼ cup green chili mixture. Bring to a boil; reduce heat to medium. Simmer, uncovered 5 minutes, stirring occasionally.

3. Pour into serving bowls. Top each serving with small dollops of remaining green chili mixture and additional sour cream, if desired. Run tip of spoon through dollops to swirl.

Makes 4 servings

Omit food processor step by adding green chilies directly to soup. Finely chop cilantro and combine with sour cream. Dollop with sour cream-cilantro mixture as directed.

Nutrients per Serving: 72 Calories (17% of calories from fat),
1g Total Fat, <1g Saturated Fat, 5mg Cholesterol, 276mg Sodium,
4g Protein, 12g Carbohydrate, 4g Dietary Fiber

Spicy Pumpkin Soup with Green Chili Swirl

Hot and Sour Soup

3 cans (about 14 ounces each) chicken broth
8 ounces boneless skinless chicken breasts, cut into ¼-inch-thick strips
1 cup shredded carrots
1 cup thinly sliced mushrooms
½ cup bamboo shoots, cut into matchstick-size strips
2 tablespoons rice vinegar or white wine vinegar
½ to ¾ teaspoon white pepper
¼ to ½ teaspoon hot pepper sauce
2 tablespoons cornstarch
2 tablespoons soy sauce
1 tablespoon dry sherry
2 medium green onions, sliced
1 egg, slightly beaten

Combine chicken broth, chicken, carrots, mushrooms, bamboo shoots, vinegar, pepper and hot pepper sauce in large saucepan. Bring to a boil over medium-high heat; reduce heat to low. Cover; simmer about 5 minutes or until chicken is no longer pink in center.

Stir together cornstarch, soy sauce and sherry in small bowl until smooth. Add to chicken broth mixture. Cook and stir until mixture comes to a boil. Stir in green onions and egg. Cook about 1 minute, stirring in one direction, until egg is cooked. Ladle soup into bowls. **Makes about 7 cups or 6 side-dish servings**

Nutrients per Serving: 120 Calories (30% of calories from fat), 4g Total Fat, 1g Saturated Fat, 75mg Cholesterol, 1279mg Sodium, 13g Protein, 9g Carbohydrate, 2g Dietary Fiber

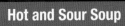
Hot and Sour Soup

Cioppino

- **1 teaspoon olive oil**
- **1 large onion, chopped**
- **1 cup sliced celery, with celery tops**
- **1 clove garlic, minced**
- **4 cups water**
- **1 fish flavor bouillon cube**
- **1 tablespoon salt-free Italian herb seasoning**
- **¼ pound cod or other boneless mild-flavored fish fillets**
- **¼ pound small shrimp, peeled and deveined**
- **¼ pound bay scallops**
- **1 large tomato, chopped**
- **¼ cup flaked crabmeat or crabmeat blend**
- **1 can (10 ounces) baby clams, rinsed and drained (optional)**
- **2 tablespoons fresh lemon juice**

1. Heat olive oil in large saucepan over medium heat until hot. Add onion, celery and garlic. Cook and stir 5 minutes or until onion is soft. Add water, bouillon cube and Italian seasoning. Cover and bring to a boil over high heat.

2. Cut cod fillets into ½-inch pieces. Add cod, shrimp, scallops and tomato to saucepan. Reduce heat to medium-low; simmer 10 to 15 minutes or until seafood is opaque. Add crabmeat, clams and lemon juice. Heat through. Garnish with lemon wedges, if desired.

Makes 4 servings

Prep and Cook Time: 30 minutes

Nutrients per Serving: 122 Calories (18% of calories from fat), 2g Total Fat, <1g Saturated Fat, 75mg Cholesterol, 412mg Sodium, 18g Protein, 8g Carbohydrate, 2g Dietary Fiber

Cioppino

Cheesy Vegetable Soup

2 teaspoons CRISCO® Oil*
¼ cup chopped green or red bell pepper
¼ cup chopped onion
2 tablespoons all-purpose flour
½ teaspoon dry mustard
⅛ teaspoon cayenne pepper
1 cup chicken broth
½ cup skim milk
1 package (10 ounces) mixed vegetables (broccoli, cauliflower and carrots) in cheese flavor sauce, thawed
1 package (9 ounces) frozen cut green beans, thawed
½ teaspoon salt

*Use your favorite Crisco Oil product.

1. Heat oil in large saucepan on medium heat. Add green pepper and onion. Cook and stir 2 to 3 minutes or until crisp-tender. Remove from heat.

2. Stir in flour, dry mustard and cayenne. Stir in broth and milk gradually. Return to heat. Cook and stir until mixture thickens.

3. Stir in vegetables in cheese sauce, green beans and salt. Simmer 5 minutes or until vegetables are tender.   **Makes 4 servings**

Nutrients per Serving (One-Fourth of Recipe): 95 Calories
(32% of calories from fat), 5g Total Fat, 1g Saturated Fat, 2mg Cholesterol,
888mg Sodium, 5g Protein, 17g Carbohydrate, 4g Dietary Fiber

Black Bean Bisque with Crab

3 cups low sodium chicken broth, defatted
1 jar (16 ounces) GUILTLESS GOURMET® Black Bean Dip (Spicy or Mild)
1 can (6 ounces) crabmeat, drained
2 tablespoons brandy (optional)
6 tablespoons low fat sour cream
   Chopped fresh chives (optional)

Microwave Directions

Combine broth and bean dip in 2-quart glass measure or microwave-safe casserole dish. Cover with vented plastic wrap or lid; microwave on HIGH (100% power) 6 minutes or until soup starts to bubble.

Stir in crabmeat and brandy, if desired; microwave on MEDIUM (50% power) 2 minutes or to desired serving temperature. To serve, ladle bisque into 8 individual ramekins or soup bowls, dividing evenly. Swirl 1 tablespoon sour cream into each serving. Garnish with chives, if desired.   **Makes 8 servings**

Stove Top Directions: Combine broth and bean dip in 2-quart saucepan; bring to a boil over medium heat. Stir in crabmeat and brandy, if desired; cook 2 minutes or to desired serving temperature. Serve as directed.

Nutrients per Serving: 104 Calories (13% of calories from fat), 1g Total Fat, 1g Saturated Fat, 25mg Cholesterol, 367mg Sodium, 11g Protein, 10g Carbohydrate, 2g Dietary Fiber

Chicken Gumbo

4 TYSON® Fresh Skinless Chicken Thighs
4 TYSON® Fresh Skinless Chicken Drumsticks
¼ cup all-purpose flour
2 teaspoons Cajun or Creole seasoning blend
2 tablespoons vegetable oil
1 large onion, chopped
1 cup thinly sliced celery
3 cloves garlic, minced
1 can (14½ ounces) stewed tomatoes, undrained
1 can (14½ ounces) chicken broth
1 large green bell pepper, cut into ½-inch pieces
½ to 1 teaspoon hot pepper sauce or to taste

PREP: CLEAN: Wash hands. Combine flour and Cajun seasonings in reclosable plastic bag. Add chicken, 2 pieces at a time; shake to coat. Reserve excess flour mixture. CLEAN: Wash hands.

COOK: In large saucepan, heat oil over medium heat. Add chicken and brown on all sides; remove and set aside. Sauté onion, celery and garlic 5 minutes. Add reserved flour mixture; cook 1 minute, stirring frequently. Add tomatoes, chicken broth, bell pepper and hot sauce. Bring to a boil. Return chicken to saucepan, cover and simmer over low heat, stirring occasionally, 30 minutes or until internal juices of chicken run clear. (Or insert instant-read meat thermometer in thickest part of chicken. Temperature should read 180°F.)

SERVE: Serve in shallow bowls, topped with hot cooked rice, if desired.

CHILL: Refrigerate leftovers immediately.   **Makes 6 to 8 servings**

PREP TIME: 10 minutes
COOK TIME: 1 hour

> **Nutrients per Serving:** 270 Calories (44% of calories from fat),
> 14g Total Fat, 2g Saturated Fat, 80mg Cholesterol, 660mg Sodium,
> 26g Protein, 11g Carbohydrate, 2g Dietary Fiber

Chicken Gumbo

Minted Melon Soup

1 cup water
1 tablespoon sugar
1½ cups fresh mint, including stems
2 fresh basil leaves
1½ cups diced cantaloupe
4 teaspoons lemon juice, divided
1½ cups diced and seeded watermelon

1. Combine water and sugar in small saucepan; mix well. Bring to a boil over medium heat. Add mint and basil; simmer 10 minutes or until reduced by two-thirds. Remove from heat; cover and let stand at least 2 hours or until cool. Strain liquid; set aside.

2. Place cantaloupe in food processor or blender; process until smooth. Add 2 tablespoons mint syrup and 2 teaspoons lemon juice. Blend to mix well. Pour into airtight container. Cover and refrigerate until cold. Repeat procedure with watermelon, 2 teaspoons mint syrup and remaining 2 teaspoons lemon juice. Discard any remaining mint syrup.

3. To serve, simultaneously pour ¼ cup of each melon soup, side by side, into serving bowl. Place 1 mint sprig in center for garnish, if desired. Repeat with remaining soup.

Makes 4 servings

Nutrients per Serving: 48 Calories (7% of calories from fat), <1g Total Fat, 0g Saturated Fat, 0mg Cholesterol, 7mg Sodium, 1g Protein, 11g Carbohydrate, 1g Dietary Fiber

Minted Melon Soup

Mediterranean Shrimp Soup

1 medium onion, chopped
½ medium green bell pepper, chopped
2 cloves garlic, minced
1 can (14½ ounces) whole tomatoes, undrained and coarsely chopped
2 cans (14½ ounces each) reduced-sodium chicken broth
1 can (8 ounces) tomato sauce
1 jar (2½ ounces) sliced mushrooms
½ cup orange juice
½ cup dry white wine (optional)
¼ cup ripe olives, sliced
2 bay leaves
1 teaspoon dried basil leaves
¼ teaspoon fennel seed, crushed
⅛ teaspoon black pepper
1 pound medium shrimp, peeled

Slow Cooker Directions

Place all ingredients except shrimp in slow cooker. Cover and cook on LOW 4 to
4½ hours or until vegetables are crisp-tender. Stir in shrimp. Cover and cook 15 to
30 minutes or until shrimp are opaque. Remove and discard bay leaves.

Makes 6 servings

Cook's Nook: For a heartier soup, add some fish. Cut 1 pound of whitefish or cod
into 1-inch pieces. Add the fish to your slow cooker 45 minutes before serving. Cover
and cook on LOW.

Nutrients per Serving: 144 Calories (19% of calories from fat),
3g Total Fat, <1g Saturated Fat, 117mg Cholesterol, 869mg Sodium,
17g Protein, 12g Carbohydrate, 2g Dietary Fiber

Mediterranean Shrimp Soup

Kale Soup

4 cups defatted low sodium chicken broth*
4 cups chopped kale
1 cup julienned fennel
1 cup julienned carrots
½ cup chopped onion
½ teaspoon thyme leaves, crushed
⅛ teaspoon black pepper

*To defat chicken broth, skim fat from surface of broth with spoon. Or, place can of broth in refrigerator at least 2 hours ahead of time. Before using, remove fat that has hardened on surface of broth.

Combine chicken broth, kale, fennel, carrots, onion, thyme and pepper in stockpot; bring to a boil over high heat. Reduce heat to low. Simmer, uncovered, 10 minutes.

Makes 4 servings

Nutrients per Serving: 64 Calories (12% of calories from fat), 1g Total Fat, 0g Saturated Fat, 0mg Cholesterol, 90mg Sodium, 4g Protein, 11g Carbohydrate, 4g Dietary Fiber

Ham and Beer Cheese Soup

1 cup chopped onion
½ cup sliced celery
2 tablespoons butter or margarine
1 cup hot water
1 HERB-OX® chicken flavor bouillon cube *or* 1 teaspoon instant chicken bouillon
3 cups half-and-half
3 cups (18 ounces) diced CURE 81® ham
1 (16-ounce) loaf pasteurized process cheese spread, cubed
1 (12-ounce) can beer
3 tablespoons all-purpose flour
Popcorn (optional)

In Dutch oven over medium-high heat, sauté onion and celery in butter until tender. In small liquid measuring cup, combine water and bouillon; set aside. Add half-and-half, ham, cheese, beer and ¾ cup broth to onion and celery mixture. Cook, stirring constantly, until cheese melts. Combine remaining ¼ cup broth and flour; stir until smooth. Add flour mixture to soup, stirring constantly. Cook, stirring constantly, until slightly thickened. Sprinkle individual servings with popcorn, if desired.

Makes 8 servings

Nutrients per Serving: 471 Calories (67% of calories from fat), 35g Total Fat, 20g Saturated Fat, 128mg Cholesterol, 1621mg Sodium, 29g Protein, 11g Carbohydrate, <1g Dietary Fiber

Gazpacho

1 jar (26 to 28 ounces) RAGÚ® Light Pasta Sauce
1 medium cucumber, peeled, seeded and finely chopped
1 small onion, finely chopped
1 medium green bell pepper, finely chopped
1 medium carrot, finely chopped
1 cup water
⅓ cup red wine vinegar
¼ cup olive or vegetable oil
1 tablespoon chopped fresh parsley
¼ to ½ teaspoon hot pepper sauce

1. In large nonaluminum bowl, combine all ingredients.

2. Season, if desired, with salt and ground black pepper.

3. Cover with plastic wrap and refrigerate 1 hour or until ready to serve.

Makes 10 servings

Tip: Using a food processor will save time but make sure to leave small bits of vegetables for a chunky soup.

Prep Time: 20 minutes
Cook Time: 1 hour

Nutrients per Serving: 90 Calories (54% of calories from fat),
5g Total Fat, <1g Saturated Fat, 0mg Cholesterol, 222mg Sodium,
2g Protein, 9g Carbohydrate, 2g Dietary Fiber

Roman Spinach Soup

    6 cups ⅓-less-salt chicken broth
    1 cup cholesterol-free egg substitute
    ¼ cup minced fresh basil
    3 tablespoons freshly grated Parmesan cheese
    2 tablespoons lemon juice
    1 tablespoon minced fresh parsley
    ¼ teaspoon white pepper
    ⅛ teaspoon ground nutmeg
    8 cups fresh spinach, washed, stems removed, chopped

1. Bring broth to a boil in 4-quart saucepan over medium heat.

2. Beat together egg substitute, basil, Parmesan cheese, lemon juice, parsley, white pepper and nutmeg in small bowl. Set aside.

3. Stir spinach into broth; simmer 1 minute. Slowly pour egg mixture into broth mixture, whisking constantly so egg threads form. Simmer 2 to 3 minutes or until egg is cooked. Garnish with lemon slices, if desired. Serve immediately.

Makes 8 (¾-cup) servings

Note: Soup may look curdled.

Nutrients per Serving: 46 Calories (22% of calories from fat),
1g Total Fat, 0g Saturated Fat, 2mg Cholesterol, 153mg Sodium,
6g Protein, 4g Carbohydrate, 1g Dietary Fiber

Roman Spinach Soup

Italian Sausage and Vegetable Stew

1 pound hot or mild Italian sausage links, cut into 1-inch pieces
1 package (16 ounces) frozen mixed vegetables, such as onions and green,
    red and yellow bell peppers
2 medium zucchini, sliced
1 can (14½ ounces) diced Italian-style tomatoes, undrained
1 jar (4½ ounces) sliced mushrooms, drained
4 cloves garlic, minced

1. Cook sausage in large saucepan, covered, over medium to medium-high heat 5 minutes or until browned; pour off drippings.

2. Add frozen vegetables, zucchini, tomatoes with juice, mushrooms and garlic; bring to a boil. Reduce heat and simmer, covered, 10 minutes. Cook uncovered 5 to 10 minutes or until juices have thickened slightly.   **Makes 6 (1-cup) servings**

Prep and Cook Time: 30 minutes

Nutrients per Serving: 234 Calories (19% of calories from fat),
15g Total Fat, 10g Saturated Fat, 43mg Cholesterol, 732mg Sodium,
14g Protein, 12g Carbohydrate, 2g Dietary Fiber

Italian Sausage and Vegetable Stew

From the Sea

Blackened Sea Bass

Hardwood charcoal*
2 teaspoons paprika
1 teaspoon garlic salt
1 teaspoon dried thyme leaves, crushed
¼ teaspoon white pepper
¼ teaspoon ground red pepper
¼ teaspoon black pepper
3 tablespoons butter or margarine
4 skinless sea bass or catfish fillets (4 to 6 ounces each)
Lemon halves
Fresh dill sprigs for garnish

Hardwood charcoal takes somewhat longer than regular charcoal to become hot, but results in a hotter fire than regular charcoal. A hot fire is necessary to seal in juices and cook fish quickly. If hardwood charcoal is not available, scatter dry hardwood, mesquite or hickory chunks over hot coals to create a hot fire.

1. Prepare barbecue grill for direct cooking using hardwood charcoal.

2. Meanwhile, combine paprika, garlic salt, thyme and white, red and black peppers in small bowl; mix well. Set aside. Melt butter in small saucepan over medium heat. Pour melted butter into pie plate or shallow bowl. Cool slightly.

3. Dip sea bass into melted butter, evenly coating both sides. Sprinkle both sides of sea bass evenly with paprika mixture.

4. Place sea bass on grid. (Fire will flare up when sea bass is placed on grid, but will subside when grill is covered.) Grill sea bass, on covered grill, over hot coals 4 to 6 minutes or until sea bass is blackened and flakes easily when tested with fork, turning halfway through grilling time. Serve with lemon halves. Garnish, if desired.

Makes 4 servings

Tip: A lean to moderately fatty saltwater fish, sea bass is generally available year-round. And don't worry about the salt! Saltwater fish are quite low in sodium—they have a special structure that prevents them from becoming as salty as the sea.

Nutrients per Serving: 192 Calories (52% of calories from fat), 11g Total Fat, 6g Saturated Fat, 47mg Cholesterol, 689mg Sodium, 21g Protein, 1g Carbohydrate, <1g Dietary Fiber

Blackened Sea Bass

Grilled Swordfish á l'Orange

4 swordfish, halibut or shark steaks (about 1½ pounds)
1 orange
¾ cup orange juice
1 tablespoon lemon juice
1 tablespoon sesame oil
1 tablespoon soy sauce
1 teaspoon cornstarch
Salt and black pepper to taste

Rinse swordfish and pat dry with paper towels. Grate enough orange peel to measure 1 teaspoon; set aside. Peel orange and cut into sections; set aside. Combine orange juice, lemon juice, oil and soy sauce in small bowl. Pour half of orange juice mixture into shallow glass dish. Add ½ teaspoon grated orange peel to orange juice mixture. Place fish in dish; turn to coat in mixture. Cover and allow to marinate in refrigerator at least 1 hour.

Place remaining half of orange juice mixture in small saucepan. Stir in cornstarch and remaining ½ teaspoon orange peel. Heat over medium-high heat, stirring constantly, 3 to 5 minutes or until sauce thickens; set aside.

Remove fish from marinade; discard remaining marinade. Lightly sprinkle fish with salt and pepper. Grill over medium coals 3 to 4 minutes per side or until fish is opaque and flakes easily when tested with fork. Top with reserved orange sections and orange sauce. Serve immediately. **Makes 4 servings**

Nutrients per Serving: 243 Calories (30% of calories from fat), 8g Total Fat, 2g Saturated Fat, 67mg Cholesterol, 772mg Sodium, 34g Protein, 7g Carbohydrate, 1g Dietary Fiber

Grilled Swordfish á l'Orange

Today's Slim Tuna Stuffed Tomatoes

6 medium tomatoes
1 cup dry curd cottage cheese
½ cup plain low fat yogurt
¼ cup chopped cucumber
¼ cup chopped green bell pepper
¼ cup thinly sliced radishes
¼ cup chopped green onions
½ teaspoon dried basil leaves, crushed
⅛ teaspoon garlic powder
1 can (6½ ounces) tuna, packed in water, drained and flaked
Lettuce leaves

Cut each tomato into 6 wedges, cutting to, but not through, base of each tomato. Refrigerate. In medium bowl, combine cottage cheese and yogurt; mix well. Stir in remaining ingredients except lettuce leaves. Place tomatoes on individual lettuce-lined plates; spread wedges apart. Spoon cottage cheese mixture into center of each tomato.

Makes 6 servings

Favorite recipe from **Wisconsin Milk Marketing Board**

Nutrients per Serving: 98 Calories (12% of calories from fat),
1g Total Fat, <1g Saturated Fat, 8mg Cholesterol, 48mg Sodium,
14g Protein, 9g Carbohydrate, 2g Dietary Fiber

Today's Slim Tuna Stuffed Tomatoes

Mahi-Mahi with Fresh Pineapple Salsa

1½ cups diced fresh pineapple
¼ cup finely chopped red bell pepper
¼ cup finely chopped green bell pepper
2 tablespoons chopped fresh cilantro
2 tablespoons fresh lime juice, divided
½ teaspoon red pepper flakes
½ teaspoon grated lime peel
　Nonstick cooking spray
4 mahi-mahi fillets (4 ounces each)
1 tablespoon olive oil
½ teaspoon white pepper

To prepare Pineapple Salsa, combine pineapple, red and green peppers, cilantro, 1 tablespoon lime juice, red pepper flakes and lime peel in medium bowl.

Preheat broiler. Spray rack of broiler pan with cooking spray. Rinse mahi-mahi and pat dry with paper towels. Place mahi-mahi on rack. Combine remaining 1 tablespoon lime juice and olive oil; brush on mahi-mahi.

Broil, 4 inches from heat, 2 minutes. Turn and brush second side with olive oil mixture; sprinkle with white pepper. Continue to broil 2 minutes or until mahi-mahi flakes easily when tested with fork. Serve with Pineapple Salsa. **Makes 4 servings**

Note: Pineapple Salsa may be prepared 1 to 2 days ahead and refrigerated.

Prep and Cook Time: 25 minutes

Nutrients per Serving: 168 Calories (24% of calories from fat),
5g Total Fat, 1g Saturated Fat, 83mg Cholesterol, 102mg Sodium,
22g Protein, 10g Carbohydrate, 1g Dietary Fiber

Mahi-Mahi with Fresh Pineapple Salsa

Chilled Poached Salmon with Cucumber Sauce

1 cup water
½ teaspoon chicken or fish bouillon granules
⅛ teaspoon black pepper
4 fresh or thawed frozen pink salmon fillets (about 6 ounces each)
½ cup chopped seeded peeled cucumber
⅓ cup plain low fat yogurt
2 tablespoons sliced green onion
2 tablespoons nonfat salad dressing or mayonnaise
1 tablespoon chopped fresh cilantro
1 teaspoon Dijon mustard
2 cups shredded lettuce

Combine water, bouillon granules and pepper in large skillet. Bring to a boil over high heat. Carefully place salmon in skillet; return just to a boil. Reduce heat to medium-low. Cover and simmer 8 to 10 minutes or until salmon flakes easily when tested with fork. Remove salmon. Cover and refrigerate.

Meanwhile, combine cucumber, yogurt, onion, salad dressing, cilantro and mustard in small bowl. Cover and refrigerate. Place chilled salmon fillets on lettuce-lined plates. Spoon sauce over salmon. **Makes 4 servings**

Nutrients per Serving: 223 Calories (26% of calories from fat), 6g Total Fat, 1g Saturated Fat, 89mg Cholesterol, 322mg Sodium, 36g Protein, 4g Carbohydrate, 1g Dietary Fiber

Chilled Poached Salmon with Cucumber Sauce

Trout Stuffed with Fresh Mint and Oranges

2 pan-dressed* trout (1 to 1¼ pounds each)
½ teaspoon coarse salt, such as Kosher salt
1 orange, sliced
1 cup fresh mint leaves
1 sweet onion, sliced

*A pan-dressed trout has been gutted and scaled with head and tail removed.

1. Rinse trout under cold running water; pat dry with paper towels.

2. Sprinkle cavities of trout with salt; fill each with orange slices and mint. Cover each fish with onion slices.

3. Spray 2 large sheets of foil with nonstick cooking spray. Place 1 fish on each sheet and seal using Drugstore Wrap technique.**

4. Place foil packets, seam side down, directly on medium-hot coals; grill on covered grill 20 to 25 minutes or until trout flakes easily when tested with fork, turning once.

5. Carefully open foil packets, avoiding hot steam; remove and discard orange-mint stuffing. Serve immediately. Garnish as desired.   **Makes 6 servings**

**Place food in the center of an oblong piece of heavy-duty foil, leaving at least a two-inch border around the food. Bring the two long sides together above the food; fold down in a series of locked folds, allowing for heat circulation and expansion. Fold short ends up and over again. Press folds firmly to seal the foil packet.

Nutrients per Serving: 203 Calories (24% of calories from fat),
5g Total Fat, 1g Saturated Fat, 87mg Cholesterol, 220mg Sodium,
32g Protein, 5g Carbohydrate, 1g Dietary Fiber

Trout Stuffed with Fresh Mint and Oranges

Grilled Scallops & Vegetables with Cilantro Sauce

1 teaspoon hot chili oil
1 teaspoon dark sesame oil
1 green onion, chopped
1 tablespoon finely chopped fresh ginger
1 cup ⅓-less-salt chicken broth
1 cup chopped fresh cilantro
1 pound sea scallops
2 medium zucchini, cut into ½-inch slices
2 medium yellow squash, cut into ½-inch slices
1 medium yellow onion, cut into wedges
8 large mushrooms

1. Spray cold grid with nonstick cooking spray. Preheat grill to medium-high heat. Heat chili oil and sesame oil in small saucepan over medium-low heat. Add green onion; cook about 15 seconds or just until fragrant. Add ginger; cook 1 minute.

2. Add chicken broth; bring mixture to a boil. Cook until liquid is reduced by half. Place mixture in blender or food processor with cilantro; blend until smooth. Set aside.

3. Thread scallops and vegetables onto water-soaked wooden skewers. Grill about 8 minutes per side or until scallops turn opaque. Serve hot with cilantro sauce. Garnish, if desired.

Makes 4 servings

Nutrients per Serving: 171 Calories (21% of calories from fat), 4g Total Fat, <1g Saturated Fat, 48mg Cholesterol, 258mg Sodium, 24g Protein, 11g Carbohydrate, 3g Dietary Fiber

Grilled Scallops & Vegetables with Cilantro Sauce

Halibut with Roasted Pepper Sauce

Roasted Pepper Sauce (recipe follows)
1 medium onion, thinly sliced
1 large clove garlic, minced
1 (1½-pound) halibut fillet, skinned

1. Preheat oven to 425°F. Grease shallow baking dish.

2. Prepare Roasted Pepper Sauce; set aside.

3. Cover bottom of baking dish with onion and garlic. Top with fish and sauce.

4. Bake 20 minutes or until fish flakes easily when tested with fork. Garnish as desired.   **Makes 4 servings**

Roasted Pepper Sauce

1 (7-ounce) can chopped green chilies, drained
1 (7-ounce) jar roasted red peppers, drained
⅔ cup chicken broth

Combine ingredients in food processor or blender; process until smooth.

Nutrients per Serving: 229 Calories (18% of calories from fat), 4g Total Fat, 1g Saturated Fat, 54mg Cholesterol, 547mg Sodium, 36g Protein, 6g Carbohydrate, 2g Dietary Fiber

Baked Orange Roughy with Sautéed Vegetables

2 orange roughy fillets (about 4 ounces each)
2 teaspoons olive oil
1 medium carrot, cut into matchstick pieces
4 medium mushrooms, sliced
⅓ cup chopped onion
¼ cup chopped green or yellow bell pepper
1 clove garlic, minced
Black pepper
Lemon wedges

1. Preheat oven to 350°F. Place fish fillets in shallow baking dish. Bake 15 minutes or until fish flakes easily when tested with fork.

2. Heat olive oil in small nonstick skillet over medium-high heat. Add carrots; cook 3 minutes, stirring occasionally. Add mushrooms, onion, bell pepper and garlic; cook and stir 2 minutes or until vegetables are crisp-tender.

3. Place fish on serving plates; top with vegetable mixture. Sprinkle with black pepper. Serve with lemon wedges. **Makes 2 servings**

Note: To microwave fish, place fish in shallow microwavable dish. Microwave, covered, on HIGH 2 minutes or until fish flakes easily when tested with fork. To broil fish, place fish on rack of broiler pan. Broil 4 to 6 inches from heat 4 minutes on each side or until fish flakes easily when tested with fork.

Nutrients per Serving: 157 Calories (32% of calories from fat), 6g Total Fat, 1g Saturated Fat, 22mg Cholesterol, 84mg Sodium, 18g Protein, 10g Carbohydrate, 3g Dietary Fiber

Caribbean Sea Bass with Mango Salsa

4 (4 ounces each) skinless sea bass fillets, about 1 inch thick
1 teaspoon Caribbean jerk seasoning
  Nonstick cooking spray
1 ripe mango, peeled, pitted and diced *or* **1 cup diced drained bottled mango**
2 tablespoons chopped fresh cilantro
2 teaspoons fresh lime juice
1 teaspoon minced fresh or bottled jalapeño pepper*

*Jalapeño peppers can sting and irritate the skin; wear rubber gloves when handling peppers and do not touch eyes. Wash hands after handling peppers.

1. Prepare grill or preheat broiler. Sprinkle fish with seasoning; coat lightly with cooking spray. Grill fish over medium coals or broil 5 inches from heat for 4 to 5 minutes per side or until fish flakes easily with fork.

2. Meanwhile, combine mango, cilantro, lime juice and jalapeño pepper; mix well. Serve over fish. **Makes 4 servings**

Prep Time: 10 minutes
Cook Time: 8 minutes

Nutrients per Serving: 146 Calories (15% of calories from fat), 3g Total Fat, 1g Saturated Fat, 47mg Cholesterol, 189mg Sodium, 21g Protein, 9g Carbohydrate, 1g Dietary Fiber

Caribbean Sea Bass with Mango Salsa

Grilled Snapper with Pesto

1½ cups packed fresh basil leaves
1½ cups packed fresh cilantro or parsley
 ¼ cup packed fresh mint leaves
 ¼ cup olive oil
 3 tablespoons lime juice
 3 cloves garlic, chopped
 1 tablespoon sugar
 ½ teaspoon salt
 4 (6-ounce) snapper or grouper fillets
   Black pepper

1. For pesto, combine basil, cilantro, mint, oil, lime juice, garlic, sugar and salt in food processor or blender; process until smooth.

2. Spread about ½ teaspoon pesto on each side of fillets. Sprinkle both sides with pepper to taste. Arrange fish in single layer in grill basket coated with nonstick cooking spray. Grill, covered, over medium-hot coals 3 to 4 minutes per side or until fish flakes easily when tested with fork. Serve with remaining pesto. Garnish with lime wedges if desired.   **Makes 4 servings**

Prep and Cook Time: 20 minutes

Nutrients per Serving: 305 Calories (47% of calories from fat),
16g Total Fat, 2g Saturated Fat, 62mg Cholesterol, 344mg Sodium,
34g Protein, 6g Carbohydrate, <1g Dietary Fiber

Grilled Snapper with Pesto

Crispy Oven Fried Fish Fingers

½ cup seasoned dry bread crumbs
1 tablespoon grated Parmesan cheese
2 teaspoons grated lemon peel
¾ teaspoon dried marjoram leaves
½ teaspoon paprika
¼ teaspoon dried thyme leaves
⅛ teaspoon garlic powder
4 cod fillets (about 1 pound)
3 tablespoons lemon juice
2 tablespoons dry white wine *or* water
1 tablespoon CRISCO® Oil*

Use your favorite Crisco Oil product.

1. Heat oven to 425°F. Oil 13×9×2-inch pan lightly. Place cooling rack on countertop.

2. Combine bread crumbs, Parmesan cheese, lemon peel, marjoram, paprika, thyme and garlic powder in shallow dish.

3. Rinse fish fillets. Pat dry.

4. Combine lemon juice and wine in separate shallow dish. Cut fish into desired size "fingers" or "sticks." Dip each fish finger into lemon mixture, then into crumb mixture, coating well. Place in pan. Drizzle with oil.

5. Bake at 425°F for 10 to 12 minutes or until fish flakes easily with fork. *Do not overbake.* Remove to cooling rack. Let stand 2 to 3 minutes in pan. Remove to serving plate. Garnish, if desired.   **Makes 4 servings**

Nutrients per Serving (One-Fourth of Recipe): 175 Calories
(28% of calories from fat), 6g Total Fat, 1g Saturated Fat,
60mg Cholesterol, 180mg Sodium, 24g Protein, 7g Carbohydrate,
1g Dietary Fiber

Crispy Oven Fried Fish Fingers

Marinated Citrus Shrimp

1 pound (about 32) large shrimp, peeled, tails left intact and cooked
2 oranges, peeled and cut into segments
1 can (5½ ounces) pineapple chunks in juice, drained and ¼ cup juice
    reserved
2 green onions with tops, sliced
½ cup orange juice
2 tablespoons minced fresh cilantro
2 tablespoons lime juice
2 tablespoons white wine vinegar
1 tablespoon olive or vegetable oil
1 clove garlic, minced
½ teaspoon dried basil leaves
½ teaspoon dried tarragon leaves
    White pepper (optional)

1. Combine shrimp, orange segments, pineapple chunks and green onions in resealable plastic food storage bag. Mix orange juice, reserved pineapple juice, cilantro, lime juice, vinegar, oil, garlic, basil and tarragon in medium bowl; pour over shrimp mixture, turning to coat. Season to taste with white pepper, if desired. Marinate in refrigerator 2 hours or up to 8 hours.

2. Spoon shrimp mixture onto plates. Garnish, if desired. **Makes 16 servings**

Nutrients per Serving: 51 Calories (20% of calories from fat),
1g Total Fat, <1g Saturated Fat, 44mg Cholesterol, 50mg Sodium,
5g Protein, 5g Carbohydrate, 1g Dietary Fiber

Marinated Citrus Shrimp

Broiled Hunan Fish Fillets

3 tablespoons low-sodium soy sauce
1 tablespoon finely chopped green onion
2 teaspoons dark sesame oil
1 clove garlic, minced
1 teaspoon minced fresh ginger
¼ teaspoon red pepper flakes
  Nonstick cooking spray
1 pound red snapper, scrod or cod fillets

1. Combine soy sauce, onion, oil, garlic, ginger and red pepper flakes in small bowl.

2. Spray rack of broiler pan with nonstick cooking spray. Place fish on rack; brush with soy sauce mixture.

3. Broil 4 to 5 inches from heat 10 minutes or until fish flakes easily with fork. Serve on lettuce-lined plate, if desired.   **Makes 4 servings**

Health Note: The level of pollution in today's water sources poses potential hazards to the safety of eating fish. One key to safe eating is variety—don't eat the same type of fish all the time. Another is broiling; this cooking method has been shown to reduce toxic residues if they should be present.

Nutrients per Serving: 144 Calories (24% of calories from fat),
4g Total Fat, <1g Saturated Fat, 42mg Cholesterol, 446mg Sodium,
25g Protein, 1g Carbohydrate, <1g Dietary Fiber

Broiled Hunan Fish Fillets

Baked Crab-Stuffed Trout

2 small whole trout (about 6 ounces each), cleaned and boned
3 teaspoons reduced-sodium soy sauce, divided
3 ounces frozen cooked crabmeat or imitation crabmeat, thawed, shredded
½ cup fresh bread crumbs
½ cup shredded carrot
¼ cup thinly sliced celery
¼ cup thinly sliced green onions
1 egg white, slightly beaten
2 tablespoons dry white wine
1 tablespoon grated lemon peel
1 teaspoon garlic powder
½ teaspoon black pepper
   Lemon wedges

1. Preheat oven to 375°F. Wash trout; pat dry with paper towels. Place on foil-lined baking sheet. Brush inside cavities lightly with 1½ teaspoons soy sauce.

2. Combine remaining 1½ teaspoons soy sauce, crabmeat, bread crumbs, carrot, celery, onions, egg white, wine, lemon peel, garlic powder and pepper in small bowl; blend well. Divide stuffing in half; place stuffing inside cavity of each trout.

3. Bake 30 minutes or until trout flakes easily when tested with fork. Serve with lemon wedges. Garnish, if desired.   **Makes 4 servings**

Nutrients per Serving: 108 Calories (17% of calories from fat), 2g Total Fat, <1g Saturated Fat, 35mg Cholesterol, 426mg Sodium, 15g Protein, 6g Carbohydrate, <1g Dietary Fiber

Baked Crab-Stuffed Trout

Tandoori-Style Seafood Kabobs

½ pound each salmon fillet, tuna steak and swordfish steak*
1 teaspoon salt
1 teaspoon ground cumin
¼ teaspoon black pepper
 Dash ground cinnamon
 Dash ground cloves
 Dash ground nutmeg
 Dash ground cardamom (optional)
½ cup plain low-fat yogurt
¼ cup lemon juice
1 piece (1-inch cube) peeled fresh ginger, minced
1 tablespoon olive oil
2 cloves garlic, minced
½ jalapeño pepper,** seeded and minced
½ pound large shrimp, shelled with tails intact, deveined
1 each red and green bell pepper, cut into bite-size pieces
 Fresh parsley sprigs
 Fresh chives

*Any firm fish can be substituted for any fish listed above.

**Jalapeño peppers can sting and irritate the skin; wear rubber gloves when handling peppers and do not touch eyes. Wash hands after handling peppers.

Cut fish into 1½-inch cubes; cover and refrigerate. Heat salt and spices in small skillet over medium heat until fragrant (or spices may be added to marinade without heating); place spices in 2-quart glass dish. Add yogurt, lemon juice, ginger, oil, garlic and jalapeño pepper; mix well. Add fish and shrimp; turn to coat. Cover and refrigerate at least 1 hour but no longer than 2 hours. Thread a variety of seafood onto each metal or wooden skewer, alternating with bell peppers. (Soak wooden skewers in hot water 30 minutes to prevent burning.) Grill kabobs over medium-hot KINGSFORD® Briquets about 2 minutes per side until fish flakes easily when tested with fork and shrimp are pink and opaque. Remove seafood and peppers from skewers. Garnish with parsley and chives.

Makes 4 servings

Nutrients per Serving: 278 Calories (36% of calories from fat),
11g Total Fat, 4g Saturated Fat, 101mg Cholesterol, 271mg Sodium,
40g Protein, 3g Carbohydrate, 2g Dietary Fiber

Tandoori-Style Seafood Kabob

Hot and Sour Shrimp

½ **package (½ ounce) dried black Chinese mushrooms***
½ **small unpeeled cucumber**
1 **tablespoon brown sugar**
2 **teaspoons cornstarch**
3 **tablespoons rice vinegar**
2 **tablespoons low sodium soy sauce**
1 **tablespoon vegetable oil**
1 **pound medium raw shrimp, peeled and deveined**
2 **cloves garlic, minced**
¼ **teaspoon red pepper flakes**
1 **large red bell pepper, cut into short, thin strips**
  Hot cooked Chinese egg noodles (optional)

*Or substitute ¾ cup sliced fresh mushrooms. Omit step 1.

1. Place mushrooms in small bowl; cover with warm water. Soak 20 minutes to soften. Drain; squeeze out excess water. Discard stems; slice caps.

2. Cut cucumber in half lengthwise; scrape out seeds. Slice crosswise.

3. Combine brown sugar and cornstarch in small bowl. Blend in vinegar and soy sauce until smooth.

4. Heat oil in wok or large nonstick skillet over medium heat. Add shrimp, garlic and red pepper flakes; stir-fry 1 minute. Add mushrooms and bell pepper strips; stir-fry 2 minutes or until shrimp are opaque.

5. Stir vinegar mixture; add to wok. Cook and stir 30 seconds or until sauce boils and thickens. Add cucumber; stir-fry until heated through. Serve over noodles, if desired.

Makes 4 servings

Nutrients per Serving: 165 Calories (24% of calories from fat), 5g Total Fat, <1g Saturated Fat, 174mg Cholesterol, 466mg Sodium, 20g Protein, 11g Carbohydrate, 1g Dietary Fiber

Golden Apple Stuffed Fillets

 1 cup grated peeled Washington Golden Delicious apple
 ½ cup grated carrot
 ½ cup minced green onions
 2 tablespoons fresh lemon juice
 ¼ teaspoon salt
 ¼ teaspoon ground ginger
 ¼ teaspoon ground, dried mustard
 ¼ teaspoon ground black pepper
 ⅛ teaspoon dried thyme
 4 sole, cod or other white fish fillets (4 to 5 ounces each)
 ¼ cup chicken broth or water

1. Heat oven to 400°F; lightly oil small roasting pan. In medium bowl, combine apple, carrot, green onions, lemon juice, salt, ginger, mustard, pepper and thyme; mix well.

2. Spread apple mixture evenly over length of fillets; carefully roll up from shorter ends. Place stuffed fillets, seams sides down, in oiled pan. Pour broth over rolled fillets; cover with aluminum foil and bake 10 to 15 minutes or until fish is opaque and barely flakes. **Makes 4 servings**

Microwave Directions: Prepare apple stuffing mixture and roll up fillets as above. Place stuffed fillets as directed, seams side down, in oiled microwave-safe dish. Pour broth over rolled fillets; cover with waxed paper and microwave at HIGH (100% power) 5 to 7 minutes or until fish is opaque and barely flakes. (If microwave does not have carousel, rotate dish halfway through cooking.)

Favorite recipe from **Washington Apple Commission**

Nutrients per Serving: 146 Calories (10% of calories from fat),
2g Total Fat, <1g Saturated Fat, 60mg Cholesterol, 306mg Sodium,
22g Protein, 10g Carbohydrate, 2g Dietary Fiber

Snapper Veracruz

Nonstick cooking spray
1 teaspoon olive oil
¼ large onion, thinly sliced
⅓ cup low sodium fish or vegetable broth, defatted* and divided
2 cloves garlic, minced
1 cup GUILTLESS GOURMET® Roasted Red Pepper Salsa
20 ounces fresh red snapper, tilapia, sea bass or halibut fillets

To defat broth, simply chill the canned broth thoroughly. Open the can and use a spoon to lift out any solid fat floating on the surface of the broth.

Preheat oven to 400°F. Coat baking dish with cooking spray. (Dish needs to be large enough for fish to fit snugly together.) Heat oil in large nonstick skillet over medium heat until hot. Add onion; cook and stir until onion is translucent. Stir in 3 tablespoons broth. Add garlic; cook and stir 1 minute more. Stir in remaining broth and salsa. Bring mixture to a boil. Reduce heat to low; simmer about 2 minutes or until heated through.

Wash fish thoroughly; pat dry with paper towels. Place in prepared baking dish, overlapping thin edges to obtain an overall equal thickness. Pour and spread salsa mixture over fish.

Bake 15 minutes or until fish turns opaque and flakes easily when tested with fork. Serve hot.

Makes 4 servings

Nutrients per Serving: 184 Calories (16% of calories from fat), 3g Total Fat, <1g Saturated Fat, 52mg Cholesterol, 353mg Sodium, 30g Protein, 6g Carbohydrate, 0g Dietary Fiber

Snapper Veracruz

Mesquite-Grilled Salmon Fillets

2 tablespoons olive oil
1 clove garlic, minced
2 tablespoons lemon juice
1 teaspoon grated lemon peel
½ teaspoon dried dill weed
½ teaspoon dried thyme leaves
¼ teaspoon salt
¼ teaspoon black pepper
4 salmon fillets, ¾ to 1 inch thick (about 5 ounces each)

Cover 1 cup mesquite chips with cold water; soak 20 to 30 minutes. Prepare grill for direct cooking.

Combine oil and garlic in small microwavable bowl. Microwave at HIGH 1 minute or until garlic is tender. Add lemon juice, lemon peel, dill, thyme, salt and pepper; whisk until blended. Brush skinless sides of salmon with half of lemon mixture.

Drain mesquite chips; sprinkle chips over coals. Place salmon, skin side up, on grid. Grill, covered, over medium-high heat 4 to 5 minutes; turn and brush with remaining lemon mixture. Grill 4 to 5 minutes or until salmon flakes easily when tested with fork.

Makes 4 servings

Nutrients per Serving: 225 Calories (48% of calories from fat), 12g Total Fat, 4g Saturated Fat, 72mg Cholesterol, 226mg Sodium, 28g Protein, 1g Carbohydrate, <1g Dietary Fiber

Mesquite-Grilled Salmon Fillet

Baked Cod with Tomatoes and Olives

1 pound cod fillets (about 4 fillets), cut into 2-inch pieces
1 can (14½ ounces) diced Italian-style tomatoes, drained
2 tablespoons chopped pitted ripe olives
1 teaspoon bottled minced garlic
2 tablespoons chopped fresh parsley

1. Preheat oven to 400°F. Spray 13×9-inch baking dish with nonstick olive oil-flavored cooking spray. Arrange cod fillets in pan; season to taste with salt and pepper.

2. Combine tomatoes, olives and garlic in medium bowl. Spoon over fish.

3. Bake 20 minutes or until fish flakes when tested with a fork. Sprinkle with parsley.

Makes 4 servings

Prep and Cook Time: 25 minutes

Nutrients per Serving: 133 Calories (14% of calories from fat),
2g Total Fat, <1g Saturated Fat, 48mg Cholesterol, 429mg Sodium,
21g Protein, 5g Carbohydrate, 1g Dietary Fiber

Baked Cod with Tomatoes and Olives

Mediterranean Mahimahi with Creamy Herb Sauce

Creamy Herb Sauce (recipe follows)
¼ cup lemon juice
2 tablespoons olive oil
1½ teaspoons grated lemon peel
½ teaspoon dried oregano leaves
¼ teaspoon salt
¼ teaspoon black pepper
1¼ pounds mahimahi, ½ to ¾ inch thick, cut into 4 or 5 pieces

Prepare Creamy Herb Sauce; cover and refrigerate.

Combine lemon juice, oil, lemon peel, oregano, salt and pepper in small bowl until blended. Place juice mixture and mahimahi in large resealable plastic food storage bag. Close bag securely, turning to coat. Marinate in refrigerator 30 minutes, turning after 15 minutes.

Prepare grill for direct cooking.

Drain mahimahi; reserve marinade. Place mahimahi on grid. Grill, covered, over medium-high heat 4 to 5 minutes; turn and brush with reserved marinade. Grill 4 to 5 minutes or until mahimahi flakes easily when tested with fork. Serve with Creamy Herb Sauce.   **Makes 4 to 5 servings**

Creamy Herb Sauce

½ cup plain yogurt
½ cup chopped peeled cucumber
1 tablespoon chopped fresh basil
1 teaspoon dried oregano leaves
½ teaspoon dried mint leaves
¼ teaspoon minced garlic
3 dashes ground red pepper

Combine all ingredients in small bowl until blended. Cover and refrigerate 1 hour before serving.   **Makes about 1 cup**

Nutrients per Serving: 208 Calories (35% of calories from fat), 8g Total Fat, 1g Saturated Fat, 105mg Cholesterol, 278mg Sodium, 28g Protein, 4g Carbohydrate, <1g Dietary Fiber

Mediterranean Mahimahi with Creamy Herb Sauce

Hot Shrimp with Cool Salsa

¼ cup prepared salsa
4 tablespoons fresh lime juice, divided
1 teaspoon honey
1 clove garlic, minced
2 to 4 drops hot pepper sauce
1 pound large shrimp, peeled and deveined, with tails intact
1 cup finely diced honeydew melon
½ cup finely diced unpeeled cucumber
2 tablespoons minced parsley
1 green onion, finely chopped
1½ teaspoons sugar
1 teaspoon olive oil
¼ teaspoon salt

1. To make marinade, combine prepared salsa, 2 tablespoons lime juice, honey, garlic and hot pepper sauce in small bowl. Thread shrimp onto water-soaked wooden skewers. Brush shrimp with marinade; set aside.

2. To make salsa, combine remaining 2 tablespoons lime juice, melon, cucumber, parsley, onion, sugar, oil and salt in medium bowl; mix well.

3. Grill shrimp over medium coals 4 to 5 minutes or until shrimp are opaque, turning once. Serve with salsa.   **Makes 4 servings**

Nutrients per Serving: 132 Calories (15% of calories from fat),
2g Total Fat, <1g Saturated Fat, 175mg Cholesterol, 398mg Sodium,
19g Protein, 8g Carbohydrate, 1g Dietary Fiber

Hot Shrimp with Cool Salsa

Grilled Swordfish with Pineapple Salsa

1 tablespoon lime juice
2 cloves garlic, minced
4 swordfish steaks (5 ounces each)
½ teaspoon chili powder or black pepper
Pineapple Salsa (recipe follows)

1. Combine lime juice and garlic on plate. Dip swordfish in juice; sprinkle with chili powder.

2. Spray cold grid with nonstick cooking spray. Adjust grid 4 to 6 inches above heat. Preheat grill to medium-high heat. Grill fish, covered, 2 to 3 minutes. Turn over; grill 1 to 2 minutes more or until just opaque in center and still very moist. Top each serving with about 3 tablespoons Pineapple Salsa. **Makes 4 servings**

Pineapple Salsa

½ cup finely chopped fresh pineapple
¼ cup finely chopped red bell pepper
1 green onion, thinly sliced
2 tablespoons lime juice
½ jalapeño pepper,* seeded, minced
1 tablespoon chopped fresh cilantro or fresh basil

*Jalapeño peppers can sting and irritate the skin; wear rubber gloves when handling peppers and do not touch eyes. Wash hands after handling peppers.

1. Combine all ingredients in small nonmetallic bowl. Serve at room temperature.
Makes 4 servings

Nutrients per Serving: 194 Calories (28% of calories from fat),
6g Total Fat, 2g Saturated Fat, 56mg Cholesterol, 183mg Sodium,
28g Protein, 6g Carbohydrate, 1g Dietary Fiber

Grilled Swordfish with Pineapple Salsa

Plentiful Poultry

Sassy Chicken & Peppers

- **2 teaspoons Mexican seasoning***
- **2 (4-ounce) boneless skinless chicken breasts**
- **2 teaspoons canola oil**
- **1 small red onion, sliced**
- **½ red bell pepper, cut into long thin strips**
- **½ yellow or green bell pepper, cut into long, thin strips**
- **¼ cup chunky salsa or chipotle salsa**
- **1 tablespoon lime juice**
- **Lime wedges (optional)**

If Mexican seasoning is not available, substitute 1 teaspoon chili powder, ½ teaspoon ground cumin, ½ teaspoon salt and ⅛ teaspoon ground red pepper.

1. Sprinkle seasonings over both sides of chicken.

2. Heat oil in large nonstick skillet over medium heat. Add onion; cook 3 minutes, stirring occasionally.

3. Add bell pepper strips; cook 3 minutes, stirring occasionally.

4. Push vegetables to edges of skillet; add chicken to skillet. Cook 5 minutes; turn. Stir salsa and lime juice into vegetables. Continue to cook 4 minutes or until chicken is no longer pink in the center and vegetables are tender.

5. Transfer chicken to serving plates; top with vegetable mixture and garnish with lime wedges, if desired. **Makes 2 servings**

Nutrients per Serving: 224 Calories (31% of calories from fat), 8g Total Fat, 1g Saturated Fat, 69mg Cholesterol, 813mg Sodium, 27g Protein, 11g Carbohydrate, 3g Dietary Fiber

Sassy Chicken & Peppers

Thai Grilled Chicken

4 boneless chicken breast halves, skinned if desired (about 1¼ pounds)
¼ cup soy sauce
2 teaspoons bottled minced garlic
½ teaspoon red pepper flakes
2 tablespoons honey
1 tablespoon fresh lime juice

1. Prepare grill for grilling. Place chicken in shallow dish or plate. Combine soy sauce, garlic and pepper flakes in measuring cup. Pour over chicken, turning to coat. Let stand 10 minutes.

2. Meanwhile, combine honey and lime juice in small bowl until blended; set aside.

3. Place chicken on grid over medium coals; brush with some of marinade remaining in dish. Discard remaining marinade. Grill over covered grill 5 minutes. Brush chicken with half of honey mixture; turn and brush with remaining honey mixture. Grill 5 minutes more or until chicken is cooked through.   **Makes 4 servings**

Prep/Cook Time: 25 minutes

Nutrients per Serving: 146 Calories (7% of calories from fat),
1g Total Fat, <1g Saturated Fat, 53mg Cholesterol, 1077mg Sodium,
22g Protein, 11g Carbohydrate, <1g Dietary Fiber

Chicken Tikka
(Tandoori-Style Grilled Chicken)

2 chickens (3 pounds each), cut up
1 pint nonfat yogurt
½ cup *Frank's® RedHot® * Cayenne Pepper Sauce
1 tablespoon grated peeled fresh ginger
3 cloves garlic, minced
1 tablespoon paprika
1 tablespoon cumin seeds, crushed *or* 1½ teaspoons ground cumin
2 teaspoons salt
1 teaspoon ground coriander

Remove skin and visible fat from chicken pieces. Rinse with cold water and pat dry. Randomly poke chicken all over with the tip of sharp knife. Place chicken in resealable plastic food storage bags or large glass bowl. Combine yogurt, **Frank's RedHot** Sauce, ginger, garlic, paprika, cumin, salt and coriander in small bowl; mix well. Pour over chicken pieces, turning pieces to coat evenly. Seal bags or cover bowl and marinate in refrigerator 1 hour or overnight.

Place chicken on oiled grid, reserving marinade. Grill over medium coals 45 minutes or until chicken is no longer pink near bone and juices run clear, turning and basting often with marinade. (Do not baste during last 10 minutes of cooking.) Discard any remaining marinade. Serve warm.

Makes 6 to 8 servings

Prep Time: 15 minutes
Marinate Time: 1 hour
Cook Time: 45 minutes

Nutrients per Serving: 746 Calories (62% of calories from fat), 50g Total Fat, 14g Saturated Fat, 238mg Cholesterol, 1145mg Sodium, 61g Protein, 8g Carbohydrate, 1g Dietary Fiber

Thai Grilled Chicke

Chicken Tikka (Tandoori-Style Grilled Chicken)

Grilled Honey Mustard Chicken with Toasted Almonds

¼ cup GREY POUPON® Dijon Mustard
3 tablespoons honey
1 tablespoon lemon juice
1 clove garlic, crushed
8 boneless skinless chicken breasts (about 2 pounds)
¼ cup PLANTERS® Sliced Almonds, toasted

1. Blend mustard, honey, lemon juice and garlic in small bowl.

2. Grill or broil chicken 6 inches from heat source for 10 to 15 minutes, turning occasionally and brushing with mustard mixture frequently. Sprinkle with almonds before serving. **Makes 8 servings**

Nutrients per Serving: 178 Calories (15% of calories from fat), 3g Total Fat, 1g Saturated Fat, 66mg Cholesterol, 256mg Sodium, 27g Protein, 8g Carbohydrate, 1g Dietary Fiber

Quick Coriander Chicken Breasts

3 tablespoons low-sodium soy sauce
1 tablespoon ground coriander
1 tablespoon red wine vinegar
1 teaspoon brown sugar
2 cloves garlic, minced
½ teaspoon ground black pepper
¼ teaspoon poultry seasoning
4 boneless, skinless chicken breast halves (about 1½ pounds)
1 tablespoon olive oil

Combine soy sauce, coriander, vinegar, brown sugar, garlic, pepper and poultry seasoning in large bowl. Add chicken, turning to coat. Heat oil in large skillet over medium heat until hot. Add chicken; cook 7 minutes. Turn chicken over; pour any remaining sauce mixture over chicken. Cook about 7 minutes more or until chicken is no longer pink in center. Serve immediately. **Makes 4 servings**

Favorite recipe from **National Chicken Council**

Nutrients per Serving: 185 Calories (34% of calories from fat), 7g Total Fat, 1g Saturated Fat, 73mg Cholesterol, 428mg Sodium, 28g Protein, 3g Carbohydrate, 0g Dietary Fiber

Fresh Herb Baked Drumsticks

8 TYSON® Individually Fresh Frozen® Chicken Drumsticks
¼ cup chicken broth
¼ cup wine vinegar
2 tablespoons corn oil
2 tablespoons chopped fresh parsley
2 tablespoons chopped fresh chives
½ teaspoon chopped fresh thyme
½ teaspoon chopped fresh marjoram
½ teaspoon salt
¼ teaspoon coarsely ground black pepper
¼ teaspoon ground cumin

PREP: Preheat oven to 400°F. Line 13×9-inch baking pan with foil; spray with nonstick cooking spray. CLEAN: Wash hands. Remove protective ice glaze from frozen chicken by holding under cool running water 1 to 2 minutes. Arrange chicken in single layer in prepared pan. CLEAN: Wash hands.

COOK: Bake 20 minutes; drain and discard juices. Combine remaining ingredients. Pour mixture over chicken. Bake 20 minutes. Turn chicken over and baste with juices. Bake 15 to 20 minutes or until internal juices of chicken run clear. (Or insert instant-read meat thermometer in thickest part of chicken. Temperature should read 180°F.)

SERVE: Serve with mashed potatoes and green beans, if desired.

CHILL: Refrigerate leftovers immediately.   **Makes 4 servings**

PREP TIME: 10 minutes
COOK TIME: 1 hour

Nutrients per Serving: 200 Calories (65% of calories from fat),
14g Total Fat, 4g Saturated Fat, 90mg Cholesterol, 630mg Sodium,
18g Protein, 1g Carbohydrate, <1g Dietary Fiber

Quick Orange Chicken

2 tablespoons frozen orange juice concentrate
1 tablespoon no-sugar-added orange marmalade
1 teaspoon Dijon mustard
¼ teaspoon salt
4 boneless skinless chicken breasts (about 14 ounces)
½ cup fresh orange sections
2 tablespoons chopped fresh parsley

1. For sauce, combine juice concentrate, marmalade, mustard and salt in 8-inch shallow round microwavable dish until juice concentrate is thawed.

2. Add chicken, coating both sides with sauce. Arrange chicken around edge of dish without overlapping. Do not overlap. Cover with vented plastic wrap. Microwave at HIGH 3 minutes; turn chicken over. Microwave at MEDIUM-HIGH (70%) 4 minutes, or until chicken is no longer pink in center.

3. Remove chicken to serving plate. Microwave remaining sauce at HIGH 2 to 3 minutes or until slightly thickened.

4. To serve, spoon sauce over chicken; top with orange sections and parsley.

Makes 4 servings

Nutrients per Serving: 157 Calories (16% of calories from fat),
3g Total Fat, 1g Saturated Fat, 60mg Cholesterol, 207mg Sodium,
23g Protein, 10g Carbohydrate, 1g Dietary Fiber

Quick Orange Chicken

Roasted Rosemary-Lemon Chicken

1 whole chicken (3¼ pounds)
1 lemon, cut into eighths
¼ cup parsley sprigs
4 sprigs rosemary
3 leaves fresh sage
2 sprigs thyme
½ teaspoon black pepper
1 can (about 14 ounces) chicken broth
1 cup sliced onion
6 cloves garlic
1 cup thinly sliced carrots
1 cup thinly sliced zucchini

1. Preheat oven to 350°F. Trim fat from chicken. Rinse chicken and pat dry with paper towels. Fill cavity of chicken with lemon, parsley, rosemary, sage, thyme and pepper. Close cavity with skewers.

2. Combine chicken broth, onion and garlic in heavy roasting pan. Place chicken in broth mixture. Roast chicken, basting occasionally with broth mixture, 1½ hours or until internal temperature reaches 180°F when tested with meat thermometer inserted into thickest part of thigh not touching any bone. Remove chicken to serving platter.

3. Combine carrots and zucchini in small saucepan. Add ¼ cup water; bring to a boil over high heat. Reduce heat to medium and cook, covered, 4 minutes or until vegetables are crisp-tender. Drain.

4. Remove skewers from chicken. Discard lemon and herbs. Remove skin. Cut chicken into pieces. Remove onion and garlic from pan with slotted spoon to medium bowl. Add carrots and zucchini; mix well. Arrange vegetable mixture around chicken. Garnish with fresh rosemary and lemon, if desired.   **Makes 6 servings**

Nutrients per Serving: 282 Calories (32% of calories from fat),
10g Total Fat, 3g Saturated Fat, 191mg Cholesterol, 338mg Sodium,
32g Protein, 8g Carbohydrate, 2g Dietary Fiber

Roasted Rosemary-Lemon Chicken

Picnic Chicken Slaw

 1 can (10¾ ounces) reduced-fat cream of chicken soup
 ⅓ cup red wine vinegar
 ¼ cup plain nonfat yogurt
 2 cloves garlic
 ½ teaspoon sugar
 ½ teaspoon salt
 ½ teaspoon black pepper
 4 cups shredded green cabbage
 2 cups shredded red cabbage
 1½ cups chopped, cooked chicken breast
 ½ cup seeded, chopped tomato
 ½ cup shredded carrots
 ½ cup sliced green onions
 ½ cup chopped peeled cucumber

Combine soup, vinegar, yogurt, garlic, sugar, salt and pepper in food processor; process until smooth. Set aside.

Combine green cabbage, red cabbage, chicken, tomato, carrots, green onions and cucumber in large bowl. Add soup mixture and toss well to coat. Refrigerate at least 2 hours to blend flavors.   **Makes 6 servings**

Nutrients per Serving: 126 Calories (21% of calories from fat),
3g Total Fat, 1g Saturated Fat, 34mg Cholesterol, 643mg Sodium,
13g Protein, 12g Carbohydrate, 3g Dietary Fiber

Picnic Chicken Slaw

No Tomato Barbecued Chicken

3 tablespoons butter or margarine
1 tablespoon minced onion
¼ cup lemon juice
1½ teaspoons mustard
1 teaspoon salt
1 teaspoon brown sugar
1 teaspoon Worcestershire sauce
¼ teaspoon ground black pepper
⅛ teaspoon hot pepper sauce
⅓ cup water
6 chicken leg-thigh combinations

Melt butter in small saucepan over medium-high heat until hot. Add onion; cook and stir about 5 minutes or until tender. Stir in lemon juice, mustard, salt, brown sugar, Worcestershire, pepper and pepper sauce. Slowly add water; stir until mixture boils. Remove from heat. Brush chicken with sauce. Place chicken on prepared grill, skin sides up, about 8 inches from heat. Grill, turning and basting with sauce every 15 minutes, 60 to 70 minutes or until fork can be inserted into chicken with ease and juices run clear, not pink. Serve immediately.   **Makes 6 servings**

Favorite recipe from **National Chicken Council**

Nutrients per Serving: 311 Calories (58% of calories from fat), 20g Total Fat, 9g Saturated Fat, 119mg Cholesterol, 273mg Sodium, 29g Protein, 2g Carbohydrate, <1g Dietary Fiber

Lemon-Garlic Chicken

2 tablespoons olive oil
2 cloves garlic, pressed
1 teaspoon grated lemon peel
1 teaspoon lemon juice
¼ teaspoon salt
¼ teaspoon black pepper
4 skinless boneless chicken breast halves (about 1 pound)

Combine oil, garlic, lemon peel, lemon juice, salt and pepper in small bowl. Brush oil mixture over both sides of chicken to coat. Lightly oil grid to prevent sticking. Grill chicken over medium KINGSFORD® Briquets 8 to 10 minutes or until chicken is no longer pink in center, turning once.   **Makes 4 servings**

Nutrients per Serving: 199 Calories (45% of calories from fat), 10g Total Fat, 1g Saturated Fat, 70mg Cholesterol, 208mg Sodium, 26g Protein, 1g Carbohydrate, <1g Dietary Fiber

Zesty Caribbean Chicken Breasts

¼ cup CRISCO® Oil*
1 teaspoon grated lemon peel
¼ cup lemon juice
1 tablespoon paprika
1 tablespoon honey
1 teaspoon garlic salt
1 teaspoon ginger
1 teaspoon dried oregano leaves
¼ teaspoon hot pepper sauce
6 boneless, skinless chicken breast halves (about 1½ pounds)

*Use your favorite Crisco Oil product.

1. Combine oil, lemon peel, lemon juice, paprika, honey, garlic salt, ginger, oregano and hot pepper sauce in shallow baking dish. Stir well. Add chicken. Turn to coat. Refrigerate 30 minutes or up to 4 hours, turning occasionally.

2. Heat broiler or prepare grill.

3. Remove chicken from lemon juice mixture. Broil or grill 3 to 5 minutes per side or until chicken is no longer pink in center. **Makes 6 servings**

Nutrients per Serving (One-Sixth of Recipe): 170 Calories (30% of calories from fat), 6g Total Fat, 1g Saturated Fat, 65mg Cholesterol, 230mg Sodium, 26g Protein, 2g Carbohydrate, <1g Dietary Fiber

Spinach-Stuffed Chicken Breasts

2 boneless skinless chicken breasts (8 ounces each), halved
5 ounces frozen chopped spinach, thawed and well drained
2 tablespoons freshly grated Parmesan cheese
1 teaspoon grated lemon peel
¼ teaspoon black pepper
   Olive oil-flavored nonstick cooking spray
1 cup thinly sliced mushrooms
6 slices (2 ounces) thinly sliced low fat turkey-ham
1 cup white grape juice

1. Trim fat from chicken; discard. Place each chicken breast between 2 sheets of plastic wrap. Pound with meat mallet until chicken is about ¼ inch thick.

2. Preheat oven to 350°F. Pat spinach dry with paper towels. Combine spinach, Parmesan, lemon peel and black pepper in large bowl. Spray small nonstick skillet with cooking spray; add mushrooms. Cook and stir over medium heat 3 to 4 minutes or until tender.

3. Arrange 1½ slices turkey-ham over each chicken breast. Spread each with one-fourth of spinach mixture. Top each with mushrooms. Beginning with longer side, roll chicken tightly. Tie with kitchen string.

4. Place stuffed chicken breasts in 9-inch square baking pan, seam side down. Lightly spray chicken with cooking spray. Pour white grape juice over top. Bake 30 minutes or until chicken is no longer pink.

5. Remove string; cut chicken rolls into ½-inch diagonal slices. Arrange on plate. Pour pan juices over chicken. Garnish as desired.   **Makes 4 servings**

Nutrients per Serving: 187 Calories (21% of calories from fat),
4g Total Fat, 2g Saturated Fat, 71mg Cholesterol, 302mg Sodium,
26g Protein, 10g Carbohydrate, 2g Dietary Fiber

Spinach-Stuffed Chicken Breast

Spicy Island Chicken

1 cup finely chopped white onion
⅓ cup white wine vinegar
6 green onions, finely chopped
6 cloves garlic, minced
1 habañero or serrano pepper,* finely chopped
4½ teaspoons olive oil
4½ teaspoons fresh thyme leaves *or* 2 teaspoons dried thyme leaves
1 tablespoon ground allspice
2 teaspoons sugar
1 teaspoon salt
1 teaspoon ground cinnamon
1 teaspoon ground nutmeg
1 teaspoon black pepper
½ teaspoon ground red pepper
6 boneless skinless chicken breasts

Habañero peppers can sting and irritate the skin; wear rubber gloves when handling peppers and do not touch eyes. Wash hands after handling.

1. Combine all ingredients except chicken in medium bowl; mix well. Place chicken in resealable plastic food storage bag and add seasoning mixture. Seal bag; turn to coat chicken. Marinate in refrigerator 4 hours or overnight.

2. Spray cold grid with nonstick cooking spray. Adjust grid to 4 to 6 inches above heat. Preheat grill to medium-high heat.

3. Remove chicken from marinade. Grill 5 to 7 minutes per side or until chicken is no longer pink in center, brushing occasionally with marinade. *Do not brush with marinade during last 5 minutes of grilling.* Discard remaining marinade. Serve with grilled sweet potatoes. Garnish, if desired.

Makes 6 servings

Nutrients per Serving: 164 Calories (27% of calories from fat), 5g Total Fat, 1g Saturated Fat, 69mg Cholesterol, 256mg Sodium, 26g Protein, 3g Carbohydrate, 1g Dietary Fiber

Spicy Island Chicken

Tasty Skillet Chicken for Two

1 tablespoon butter or margarine
2 chicken breast halves
½ cup chopped onion
1 large tomato, chopped
1 tablespoon Worcestershire sauce
½ teaspoon dry mustard
½ teaspoon salt
¼ teaspoon ground black pepper
    Hot cooked rice (optional)

Melt butter in skillet over medium-high heat until hot. Add chicken; cook 5 minutes or until brown, turning occasionally. Add onion; cook 2 minutes or until onion is tender. Add tomato, Worcestershire, mustard, salt and pepper; bring to a boil. Reduce heat to low; cover and simmer 20 minutes or until fork can be inserted into chicken with ease and juices run clear, not pink. Serve with hot rice, if desired.   **Makes 2 servings**

Favorite recipe from **National Chicken Council**

Nutrients per Serving: 295 Calories (43% of calories from fat),
14g Total Fat, 6g Saturated Fat, 98mg Cholesterol, 800mg Sodium,
31g Protein, 11g Carbohydrate, 3g Dietary Fiber

Stir-Fried Chicken and Almonds

2 cups chicken broth
3 tablespoons soy sauce
2 tablespoons cornstarch
½ teaspoon ground ginger
1 cup diagonally sliced celery
¾ cup thinly sliced onions
¾ cup red bell pepper strips, cut into 1-inch pieces
3 tablespoons PLANTERS® Peanut Oil, divided
1½ pounds boneless, skinless chicken breasts, cut into 1-inch cubes
¾ cup PLANTERS® Sliced Almonds
Hot cooked rice (optional)

1. Mix broth, soy sauce, cornstarch and ginger in small bowl; set aside.

2. Cook and stir celery, onions and peppers in 2 tablespoons oil in large skillet over medium-high heat until tender-crisp; remove from skillet.

3. Add remaining oil to skillet; cook and stir chicken until no longer pink. Stir in broth mixture; cook and stir until mixture thickens and begins to boil.

4. Stir in vegetables and almonds. Serve over rice, if desired.   **Makes 6 servings**

Nutrients per Serving: 305 Calories (50% of calories from fat),
17g Total Fat, 2g Saturated Fat, 67mg Cholesterol, 955mg Sodium,
30g Protein, 9g Carbohydrate, 3g Dietary Fiber

Southwest Skillet

1 cup cubed cooked chicken breast
1 bag (16 ounces) BIRDS EYE® frozen Pasta Secrets Zesty Garlic
1 cup chunky salsa
½ teaspoon chili powder
½ cup chopped green or red bell pepper

- In large skillet, combine all ingredients.

- Cook over medium heat 10 to 15 minutes or until heated through.

Makes 4 servings

Cheesy Southwest Skillet: Stir in ½ cup shredded Cheddar cheese during last 5 minutes. Cook until cheese is melted.

Creamy Southwest Skillet: Remove skillet from heat. Stir in ¼ cup sour cream before serving.

Prep Time: 5 minutes
Cook Time: 15 minutes

Nutrients per Serving: 276 Calories (32% of calories from fat), 9g Total Fat, 2g Saturated Fat, 52mg Cholesterol, 706mg Sodium, 39g Protein, 4g Carbohydrate, 3g Dietary Fiber

Southwest Skillet

Chicken with Orange and Basil

Nonstick cooking spray
4 boneless skinless chicken breast halves (1½ pounds)
¾ cup fresh orange juice
½ cup dry white wine
2 tablespoons grated orange peel
½ cup sliced red onion
1 can (6 ounces) mandarin oranges, drained
¼ cup sliced fresh basil leaves *or* 2 teaspoons dried basil leaves
Crumbled blue cheese (optional)

Spray large skillet with cooking spray; heat over medium-high heat. Add chicken; cook 7 to 8 minutes on each side or until chicken is no longer pink in center. Transfer to serving plate; keep warm.

Combine orange juice, wine and orange peel in same skillet; bring to a boil. Boil 5 minutes. Stir in onion; cook and stir about 5 minutes more or until onion is tender and sauce is reduced to about ¼ cup. Reduce heat; stir in oranges and basil. Spoon sauce over chicken; sprinkle with blue cheese, if desired.   **Makes 4 servings**

Serving Suggestion: Serve with a mixed green salad and sourdough rolls, if desired.

Nutrients per Serving: 272 Calories (17% of calories from fat),
5g Total Fat, 1g Saturated Fat, 104mg Cholesterol, 93mg Sodium,
39g Protein, 12g Carbohydrate, 1g Dietary Fiber

Chicken with Orange and Basil

Oven-Crisped Chicken Breasts

8 boneless, skinless chicken breast halves (about 2 pounds)
2 egg whites
½ cup skim milk
½ cup all-purpose flour
1 tablespoon paprika
1 teaspoon dried basil leaves
½ teaspoon salt
¼ teaspoon pepper
1 cup plain dry bread crumbs
¼ cup CRISCO® Oil*

*Use your favorite Crisco Oil product.

1. Heat oven to 425°F. Place cooling rack on countertop.

2. Rinse and dry chicken.

3. Beat egg whites in large shallow dish until frothy. Beat in milk.

4. Combine flour, paprika, basil, salt and pepper in large plastic food storage bag. Place bread crumbs in another large plastic food storage bag. Shake breast halves, one or two at a time, in flour mixture, then dip in egg white mixture. Shake in crumbs.

5. Pour oil evenly into 15¼×10¼×¾-inch jelly-roll pan or other shallow pan. Place in 425°F oven for 3 or 4 minutes or until oil is hot, but not smoking. Add chicken breasts in single layer.

6. Bake at 425°F for 10 minutes. Turn chicken over. Sprinkle with any remaining crumb mixture. Bake for 5 minutes. *Do not overbake.* Remove pan to cooling rack. Serve warm. **Makes 8 servings**

Nutrients per Serving (One-Eighth of Recipe): 240 Calories
(30% of calories from fat), 8g Total Fat, <1g Saturated Fat,
66mg Cholesterol, 222mg Sodium, 29g Protein, 12g Carbohydrate,
1g Dietary Fiber

Chicken Étouffé

¼ cup vegetable oil
⅓ cup all-purpose flour
½ cup finely chopped onion
4 boneless skinless chicken breast halves (about 1¼ pounds),
    cut into ¼-inch-thick strips
1 cup chicken broth
1 medium tomato, chopped
¾ cup sliced celery
1 medium green bell pepper, chopped
2 teaspoons Creole or Cajun seasoning blend
    Hot cooked pasta (optional)

1. Heat oil in large skillet over medium heat until hot. Add flour; cook and stir
10 minutes or until dark brown. Add onion; cook and stir 2 minutes.

2. Stir in chicken, broth, tomato, celery, bell pepper and seasoning blend. Cook
8 minutes or until chicken is no longer pink in center. Serve over pasta, if desired.

Makes 6 servings

Cook's Notes: Étouffé is a traditional dish from New Orleans. This Cajun stew
usually features chicken or shellfish, bell peppers, onions and celery.

Prep and Cook Time: 25 minutes

Nutrients per Serving: 238 Calories (45% of calories from fat),
12g Total Fat, 2g Saturated Fat, 61mg Cholesterol, 292mg Sodium,
23g Protein, 9g Carbohydrate, 1g Dietary Fiber

Chicken Stir-Fry

4 boneless skinless chicken breast halves (about 1½ pounds)
2 tablespoons vegetable oil
2 tablespoons orange juice
2 tablespoons light soy sauce
1 tablespoon cornstarch
1 bag (16 ounces) BIRDS EYE® frozen Farm Fresh Mixtures Broccoli, Carrots &
   Water Chestnuts

- Cut chicken into ½-inch-thick long strips.

- In wok or large skillet, heat oil over medium-high heat.

- Add chicken; cook 5 minutes, stirring occasionally.

- Meanwhile, in small bowl, combine orange juice, soy sauce and cornstarch; blend well and set aside.

- Add vegetables to chicken; cook 5 minutes more or until chicken is no longer pink in center, stirring occasionally.

- Stir in soy sauce mixture; cook 1 minute or until heated through.

Makes 4 servings

Serving Suggestion: Serve over hot cooked rice, if desired.

Prep Time: 12 minutes
Cook Time: 5 minutes

Nutrients per Serving: 299 Calories (33% of calories from fat),
11g Total Fat, 2g Saturated Fat, 96mg Cholesterol, 422mg Sodium,
38g Protein, 11g Carbohydrate, 4g Dietary Fiber

Chicken Stir-Fry

Grilled Marinated Chicken

8 whole chicken legs (thighs and drumsticks attached) (about 3½ pounds)
6 ounces frozen lemonade concentrate, thawed
2 tablespoons white wine vinegar
1 tablespoon grated lemon peel
2 cloves garlic, minced

1. Remove skin and all visible fat from chicken. Place chicken in 13×9-inch glass baking dish. Combine remaining ingredients in small bowl; blend well. Pour over chicken; turn to coat. Cover; refrigerate 3 hours or overnight, turning occasionally.

2. Spray grid with nonstick cooking spray; prepare coals for grilling.

3. Place chicken on grill 4 inches from medium-hot coals. Grill 20 to 30 minutes or until chicken is no longer pink near bone, turning occasionally. *(Do not overcook or chicken will be dry.)* Garnish with curly endive and lemon peel strips, if desired.

Makes 8 servings

Nutrients per Serving: 169 Calories (38% of calories from fat), 7g Total Fat, 2g Saturated Fat, 77mg Cholesterol, 75mg Sodium, 22g Protein, 3g Carbohydrate, <1g Dietary Fiber

Grilled Marinated Chicken

Stuffed Chicken Breasts

4 boneless, skinless chicken breast halves (about 1 pound),
    pounded to ¼-inch thickness
½ teaspoon ground black pepper, divided
¼ teaspoon salt
1 cup cooked brown rice (cooked in chicken broth)
¼ cup minced tomato
¼ cup (1 ounce) finely shredded mozzarella cheese
3 tablespoons toasted rice bran* (optional)
1 tablespoon chopped fresh basil
  Vegetable cooking spray

To toast rice bran, spread on baking sheet and bake at 325°F. for 7 to 8 minutes.

Season insides of chicken breasts with ¼ teaspoon pepper and salt. Combine rice, tomato, cheese, bran, basil, and remaining ¼ teaspoon pepper. Spoon rice mixture on top of pounded chicken breasts; fold over and secure sides with water-soaked wooden toothpicks. Wipe off outsides of chicken breasts with paper towel. Coat a large skillet with cooking spray and place over medium-high heat until hot. Cook stuffed chicken breasts 1 minute on each side or just until golden brown. Transfer chicken to shallow baking pan. Bake at 350°F. for 8 to 10 minutes.   **Makes 4 servings**

Favorite recipe from **USA Rice Federation**

Nutrients per Serving: 223 Calories (20% of calories from fat), 5g Total Fat, 1g Saturated Fat, 79mg Cholesterol, 337mg Sodium, 30g Protein, 12g Carbohydrate, 1g Dietary Fiber

Stuffed Chicken Breasts

Seared Lemon-Pepper Chicken with Pineapple Sambal

   Pineapple Sambal (recipe follows)
   1 pound chicken tenders
   2 tablespoons lemon juice
   ½ teaspoon black pepper
   ¼ teaspoon ground red pepper
   ¼ teaspoon white pepper
   Nonstick cooking spray

1. Prepare Pineapple Sambal.

2. Place chicken in medium bowl with lemon juice; turn chicken to coat with juice.

3. Lift tenders from juice and lay in single layer on plate. Sprinkle with black, red and white pepper on both sides. Spray large nonstick skillet with cooking spray; heat over medium-high heat. Add ⅓ of the tenders; cook 1½ to 2 minutes or until golden. Turn; cook 1½ to 2 minutes more or until no longer pink in center. Transfer to serving platter; cover to keep warm. Repeat with remaining chicken. Serve with Pineapple Sambal; garnish with chopped fresh cilantro or basil if desired.   **Makes 4 servings**

Pineapple Sambal

   ⅔ cup chopped fresh pineapple
   ¼ cup minced red onion
   ¼ cup diced red bell pepper
   1 jalapeño pepper,* stemmed, seeded and minced
   2 tablespoons lime juice
   2 cloves garlic, minced

*Jalapeño peppers can sting and irritate the skin; wear rubber gloves when handling peppers and do not touch eyes. Wash hands after handling peppers.

Combine all ingredients in small bowl.   **Makes about 1½ cups**

Nutrients per Serving: 122 Calories (8% of calories from fat), 1g Total Fat, <1g Saturated Fat, 48mg Cholesterol, 306mg Sodium, 22g Protein, 7g Carbohydrate, 1g Dietary Fiber

Country Chicken and Creamy Gravy (Microwave)

CHICKEN
- ½ teaspoon paprika
- ½ teaspoon poultry seasoning
- ¼ teaspoon dried thyme leaves
- ¼ teaspoon salt
- ¼ teaspoon pepper
- 6 boneless, skinless chicken breast halves (about 1½ pounds)
- 1½ cups corn flakes, crushed to measure ½ cup

GRAVY
- 1 tablespoon CRISCO® Oil*
- 1 tablespoon all-purpose flour
- ½ cup skim milk
- ¼ cup condensed chicken broth, undiluted
- 2 tablespoons chopped fresh chives
- ¼ teaspoon salt
- ⅛ teaspoon pepper

*Use your favorite Crisco Oil product.

1. For chicken, combine paprika, poultry seasoning, thyme, salt and pepper in small bowl. Place chicken in shallow dish. Sprinkle half of seasoning mixture over chicken. Turn chicken over. Sprinkle with remaining seasoning mixture. Coat with corn flakes.

2. Place in 11¾×7½×2-inch glass microwave-safe dish with thickest portions toward outside of dish. Cover with waxed paper. Microwave at HIGH for 8 minutes or until chicken is no longer pink in center, rotating dish one half turn after 4 minutes. Remove chicken to serving platter. Keep warm.

3. For gravy, combine oil and flour in 4-cup glass measure. Stir until smooth. Add milk and broth slowly. Stir until smooth. Microwave at HIGH for 3 to 5 minutes or until thickened, stirring every 2 minutes. Stir in chives, salt and pepper. Spoon over chicken.

Makes 6 servings

Nutrients per Serving (One-Sixth of Recipe): 185 Calories (19% of calories from fat), 4g Total Fat, <1g Saturated Fat, 65mg Cholesterol, 385mg Sodium, 28g Protein, 7g Carbohydrate, <1g Dietary Fiber

Roast Chicken with Peppers

1 chicken (3 to 3½ pounds), cut into pieces
3 tablespoons olive oil, divided
1½ tablespoons chopped fresh rosemary
    or 1½ teaspoons dried rosemary, crushed
1 tablespoon fresh lemon juice
1¼ teaspoons salt, divided
¾ teaspoon freshly ground black pepper, divided
3 bell peppers (preferably 1 red, 1 yellow and 1 green)
1 medium onion

1. Heat oven to 375°F. Rinse chicken in cold water; pat dry with paper towel. Place in shallow roasting pan.

2. Combine 2 tablespoons oil, rosemary and lemon juice; brush over chicken. Sprinkle 1 teaspoon salt and ½ teaspoon pepper over chicken. Roast 15 minutes.

3. Cut bell peppers lengthwise into ½-inch-thick strips. Slice onion into thin wedges. Toss vegetables with remaining 1 tablespoon oil, ¼ teaspoon salt and ¼ teaspoon pepper. Spoon vegetables around chicken; roast until vegetables are tender and chicken is no longer pink in the center, about 40 minutes. Serve chicken with vegetables and pan juices. **Makes 6 servings**

Nutrients per Serving: 428 Calories (67% calories from fat), 32g Total Fat, 8g Saturated Fat, 118mg Cholesterol, 575mg Sodium, 29g Protein, 6g Carbohydrate, 2g Dietary Fiber

Roast Chicken with Peppers

Chicken Chop Suey

1 package (1 ounce) dried black Chinese mushrooms
3 tablespoons reduced-sodium soy sauce
1 tablespoon cornstarch
1 pound boneless skinless chicken breasts or thighs
2 cloves garlic, minced
1 tablespoon peanut or vegetable oil
½ cup thinly sliced celery
½ cup sliced water chestnuts
½ cup bamboo shoots
1 cup chicken broth
Hot cooked white rice or chow mein noodles
Thinly sliced green onions (optional)

Place mushrooms in small bowl; cover with warm water. Soak 20 minutes to soften. Drain; squeeze out excess water. Discard stems; quarter caps.

Blend soy sauce with cornstarch in cup until smooth.

Cut chicken into 1-inch pieces; toss with garlic in small bowl. Heat wok or large skillet over medium-high heat; add oil. Add chicken mixture and celery; stir-fry 2 minutes. Add water chestnuts and bamboo shoots; stir-fry 1 minute. Add broth and mushrooms; cook and stir 3 minutes or until chicken is no longer pink.

Stir soy sauce mixture and add to wok. Cook and stir 1 to 2 minutes until sauce boils and thickens. Serve over rice. Garnish with green onions.   **Makes 4 servings**

Nutrients per Serving: 208 Calories (28% of calories from fat),
6g Total Fat, 1g Saturated Fat, 58mg Cholesterol, 657mg Sodium,
25g Protein, 11g Carbohydrate, 1g Dietary Fiber

Chicken Chop Suey

Chicken Breasts Smothered in Tomatoes & Mozzarella

4 boneless skinless chicken breast halves (about 1½ pounds)
3 tablespoons olive oil, divided
1 cup chopped onions
2 teaspoons bottled minced garlic
1 can (14 ounces) Italian-style stewed tomatoes
1½ cups (6 ounces) shredded mozzarella cheese

1. Preheat broiler.

2. Pound chicken breasts between 2 pieces of plastic wrap to ¼-inch thickness using flat side of meat mallet or rolling pin.

3. Heat 2 tablespoons oil in ovenproof skillet over medium heat. Add chicken and cook about 3½ minutes per side or until no longer pink in center. Transfer to plate; cover and keep warm.

4. Heat remaining 1 tablespoon oil in same skillet over medium heat. Add onions and garlic; cook and stir 3 minutes. Add tomatoes; bring to a simmer. Return chicken to skillet, spooning onion and tomato mixture over chicken.

5. Sprinkle cheese over top. Broil 4 to 5 inches from heat until cheese is melted.

Makes 4 servings

Prep and Cook Time: 20 minutes

Nutrients per Serving: 449 Calories (% of calories from fat), 21g Total Fat, 7g Saturated Fat, 127mg Cholesterol, 477mg Sodium, 50g Protein, 12g Carbohydrate, 1g Dietary Fiber

Chicken Breasts Smothered in Tomatoes & Mozzarella

Zesty Garlic Chicken

¾ pound boneless skinless chicken breast, cut into 1-inch cubes
1 tablespoon vegetable oil
3 tablespoons lime or lemon juice
2 teaspoons Worcestershire sauce
2 teaspoons soy sauce
1 bag (16 ounces) BIRDS EYE® frozen Pasta Secrets Zesty Garlic

• In large skillet, cook and stir chicken in oil over medium heat until no longer pink in center.

• Stir in lime juice, Worcestershire and soy sauce.

• Add Pasta Secrets; stir well.

• Cover and cook 7 to 9 minutes or until vegetables are crisp-tender, stirring occasionally.   **Makes 4 servings**

Birds Eye Idea: Fill an empty squeeze bottle with vegetable oil and keep it near the stove for quick sautéing. This will allow you to use oil sparingly.

Prep Time: 5 minutes
Cook Time: 20 minutes

Nutrients per Serving: 341 Calories (38% of calories from fat),
14g Total Fat, 3g Saturated Fat, 76mg Cholesterol, 474mg Sodium,
48g Protein, 2g Carbohydrate, 1g Dietary Fiber

Chicken & Broccoli Stir-Fry with Peanuts

1½ cups fat-free reduced-sodium chicken broth, divided
2 tablespoons reduced-sodium soy sauce
1½ tablespoons cornstarch
½ teaspoon salt
¼ teaspoon ground ginger
¼ teaspoon garlic powder
  Nonstick cooking spray
½ teaspoon vegetable oil
1 pound boneless skinless chicken breast halves, cut into 2×¼-inch strips
1 cup small broccoli florets
1 cup red bell pepper strips
¼ cup chopped unsalted dry-roasted peanuts

1. Combine 1 cup chicken broth with soy sauce, cornstarch, salt, ginger and garlic powder in small container. Stir until smooth; set aside.

2. Lightly coat same skillet with cooking spray; heat to high heat until hot. Add oil; tilt to coat. Add chicken; stir fry 2 minutes, or until no longer pink. Remove chicken from skillet.

3. Add remaining ½ cup chicken broth to skillet; bring to a boil. Add broccoli and bell pepper; return to a boil. Reduce heat and simmer, covered, 2 minutes or until broccoli is crisp-tender.

4. Increase heat to high. Add chicken to skillet. Stir sauce and add to skillet. Bring to a boil; cook 1 to 2 minutes or until thickened. Stir in peanuts.

Makes 4 (1-cup) servings

Nutrients per Serving: 231 Calories (32% of calories from fat),
8g Total Fat, 2g Saturated Fat, 69mg Cholesterol, 686mg Sodium,
31g Protein, 7g Carbohydrate, 2g Dietary Fiber

Tex-Mex Pork Kabobs
with Chili Sour Cream Sauce

2¼ teaspoons chili powder, divided
1¾ teaspoons cumin, divided
¾ teaspoon garlic powder, divided
¾ teaspoon onion powder, divided
¾ teaspoon oregano, divided
1 pork tenderloin (1½ pounds), trimmed and cut into 1-inch pieces
1 cup reduced-fat sour cream
¾ teaspoon salt, divided
¼ teaspoon black pepper
1 large red bell pepper, cored, seeded and cut into small chunks
1 large green bell pepper, cored, seeded and cut into small chunks
1 large yellow bell pepper, cored, seeded and cut into small chunks

Blend 1½ teaspoons chili powder, 1 teaspoon cumin, ½ teaspoon garlic powder, ½ teaspoon onion powder and ½ teaspoon oregano in medium bowl. Add pork; toss well to coat. Cover tightly and refrigerate 2 to 3 hours.

Combine sour cream, remaining spices, ¼ teaspoon salt and pepper in small bowl. Mix well. Cover tightly and refrigerate 2 to 3 hours.

If using wooden skewers, soak in water 20 minutes before using. Preheat grill or broiler.

Toss pork with remaining ½ teaspoon salt. Thread meat and peppers onto skewers. Grill over medium-hot coals 10 minutes until meat is no longer pink in center, turning several times. If broiling, place skewers on foil-lined baking sheet. Broil 8 inches from heat 5 minutes per side until no longer pink in center, turning once. Serve immediately with sour cream sauce.   **Makes 4 to 6 servings**

Nutrients per Serving: 320 Calories (30% of calories from fat),
10g Total Fat, 5g Saturated Fat, 130mg Cholesterol, 564mg Sodium,
41g Protein, 12g Carbohydrate, 3g Dietary Fiber

Tex-Mex Pork Kabobs with Chili Sour Cream Sauce

Salisbury Steaks with Mushroom-Wine Sauce

1 pound lean ground beef sirloin
¾ teaspoon garlic salt or seasoned salt
¼ teaspoon black pepper
2 tablespoons butter or margarine
1 package (8 ounces) sliced button mushrooms *or* 2 packages (4 ounces each) sliced exotic mushrooms
2 tablespoons sweet vermouth or ruby port wine
1 jar (12 ounces) *or* 1 can (10½ ounces) beef gravy

1. Heat large heavy nonstick skillet over medium-high heat 3 minutes or until hot.* Meanwhile, combine ground sirloin, garlic salt and pepper; mix well. Shape mixture into four ¼-inch-thick oval patties.

2. Place patties in skillet as they are formed; cook 3 minutes per side or until browned. Transfer to plate. Pour off drippings.

3. Melt butter in skillet; add mushrooms. Cook and stir 2 minutes. Add vermouth; cook 1 minute. Add gravy; mix well.

4. Return patties to skillet; simmer uncovered over medium heat 2 minutes for medium or until desired doneness, turning meat and stirring sauce.

Makes 4 servings

*If pan is not heavy, use medium heat.

Note: For a special touch, sprinkle steaks with chopped parsley or chives.

Prep and Cook Time: 20 minutes

Nutrients per Serving: 341 Calories (61% of calories from fat), 23g Total Fat, 10g Saturated Fat, 88mg Cholesterol, 984mg Sodium, 24g Protein, 8g Carbohydrate, 1g Dietary Fiber

Salisbury Steaks with Mushroom-Wine Sauce

Beef Pot Roast

2½ pounds beef eye of round roast
1 can (14 ounces) fat-free reduced-sodium beef broth
2 cloves garlic
1 teaspoon herbs de Provence *or* ¼ teaspoon *each* rosemary,
    thyme, sage and savory
4 small turnips, peeled and cut into wedges
10 ounces fresh brussels sprouts, trimmed
8 ounces baby carrots
4 ounces pearl onions, skins removed
1 tablespoon water
2 teaspoons cornstarch

1. Heat large nonstick skillet over medium-high heat. Place roast, fat side down, in skillet. Cook, turning, until evenly browned. Remove roast from skillet; place in Dutch oven.

2. Pour broth into Dutch oven; bring to a boil over high heat. Add garlic and herbs de Provence. Cover and reduce heat; simmer 1½ hours.

3. Add turnips, brussels sprouts, carrots and onions to Dutch oven. Cover; cook 25 to 30 minutes or until vegetables are tender. Remove meat and vegetables and arrange on serving platter; cover with foil to keep warm.

4. Strain broth; return to Dutch oven. Stir water into cornstarch until smooth. Stir cornstarch mixture into broth. Bring to a boil over medium-high heat; cook and stir 1 minute or until thick and bubbly. Serve immediately with pot roast and vegetables. Garnish as desired.

Makes 8 servings

Nutrients per Serving: 261 Calories (30% of calories from fat), 9g Total Fat, 3g Saturated Fat, 79mg Cholesterol, 142mg Sodium, 35g Protein, 11g Carbohydrate, 2g Dietary Fiber

Beef Pot Roast

Beefy Bean & Walnut Stir-Fry

1 teaspoon vegetable oil
3 cloves garlic, minced
1 pound lean ground beef or ground turkey
1 bag (16 ounces) BIRDS EYE® frozen Cut Green Beans, thawed
1 teaspoon salt
½ cup walnut pieces

- In large skillet, heat oil and garlic over medium heat about 30 seconds.

- Add beef and beans; sprinkle with salt. Mix well.

- Cook 5 minutes or until beef is well browned, stirring occasionally.

- Stir in walnuts; cook 2 minutes more.   **Makes 4 servings**

Serving Suggestion: Serve over hot cooked egg noodles or rice, if desired.

Birds Eye Idea: When you add California walnuts to Birds Eye® vegetables, you not only add texture and a great nutty taste, but nutrition too.

Prep Time: 5 minutes
Cook Time: 7 to 10 minutes

Nutrients per Serving: 467 Calories (63% of calories from fat), 33g Total Fat, 9g Saturated Fat, 88mg Cholesterol, 645mg Sodium, 32g Protein, 11g Carbohydrate, 4g Dietary Fiber

Beefy Bean & Walnut Stir-Fry

Fragrant Beef with Garlic Sauce

1 boneless beef top sirloin steak, cut 1 inch thick (about 1¼ pounds)
⅓ cup reduced-sodium teriyaki sauce
10 large cloves garlic, peeled
½ cup defatted low-sodium beef broth
4 cups hot cooked white rice (optional)

1. Place beef in large plastic bag. Pour teriyaki sauce over beef. Close bag securely; turn to coat. Marinate in refrigerator at least 30 minutes or up to 4 hours.

2. Combine garlic and broth in small saucepan. Bring to a boil over high heat. Reduce heat to medium. Simmer, uncovered, 5 minutes. Cover and simmer 8 to 9 minutes until garlic is softened. Transfer to blender or food processor; process until smooth.

3. Meanwhile, drain beef; reserve marinade. Place beef on rack of broiler pan. Brush with half of reserved marinade. Broil 5 to 6 inches from heat 5 minutes. Turn beef over; brush with remaining marinade. Broil 5 minutes more.*

4. Slice beef thinly; serve with garlic sauce and rice, if desired. **Makes 4 servings**

Broiling time is for medium-rare doneness. Adjust time for desired doneness.

Nutrients per Serving: 212 Calories (24% of calories from fat),
6g Total Fat, 2g Saturated Fat, 67mg Cholesterol, 1106mg Sodium,
33g Protein, 6g Carbohydrate, <1g Dietary Fiber

Fragrant Beef with Garlic Sauce

Cuban Garlic & Lime Pork Chops

6 boneless pork chops, ¾ inch thick (about 1½ pounds)
2 tablespoons olive oil
2 tablespoons lime juice
2 tablespoons orange juice
2 teaspoons bottled minced garlic
½ teaspoon salt, divided
½ teaspoon red pepper flakes
2 small seedless oranges, peeled and chopped
1 medium cucumber, peeled, seeded and chopped
2 tablespoons chopped onion
2 tablespoons chopped fresh cilantro

1. Place pork in large resealable plastic food storage bag. Add oil, juices, garlic, ¼ teaspoon salt and pepper. Seal bag and shake to evenly distribute marinade; refrigerate up to 24 hours.

2. To make salsa, combine oranges, cucumber, onion and cilantro in small bowl; toss lightly. Cover and refrigerate 1 hour or overnight. Add remaining ¼ teaspoon salt just before serving.

3. Remove pork from marinade; discard marinade. Grill or broil pork 6 to 8 minutes on each side or until pork is no longer pink in center. Serve with salsa.

Makes 4 to 6 servings

Make-Ahead Time: 1 day before cooking
Final Prep and Cook Time: 16 minutes

Nutrients per Serving: 233 Calories (46% of calories from fat),
12g Total Fat, 3g Saturated Fat, 60mg Cholesterol, 281mg Sodium,
20g Protein, 11g Carbohydrate, 2g Dietary Fiber

Hamburger Casserole Olé

1 pound lean ground beef or ground turkey
1 package (1¼ ounces) taco seasoning mix
1 cup water
1 box (9 ounces) BIRDS EYE® frozen Cut Green Beans
½ cup shredded sharp Cheddar cheese
½ cup shredded mozzarella cheese

• Preheat oven to 325°F.

• Brown beef; drain excess fat. Add taco mix and water; cook over low heat 8 to 10 minutes or until liquid has been absorbed.

• Meanwhile, cook green beans according to package directions; drain.

• Spread meat in greased 13×9-inch baking pan. Spread beans over meat. Sprinkle with cheeses.

• Bake 15 to 20 minutes or until hot and cheese is melted.   **Makes 4 servings**

Serving Suggestion: Serve over tortillas or corn chips and top with sour cream, chopped avocado, chopped lettuce and/or chopped tomatoes.

Birds Eye Idea: Try substituting plain low-fat yogurt for sour cream in your recipes for a lighter version.

Prep Time: 15 minutes
Cook Time: 25 to 30 minutes

Nutrients per Serving: 467 Calories (60% of calories from fat), 30g Total Fat, 14g Saturated Fat, 118mg Cholesterol, 875mg Sodium, 36g Protein, 9g Carbohydrate, 2g Dietary Fiber

Italian-Style Meat Loaf

1 can (6 ounces) no-salt-added tomato paste
½ cup dry red wine plus ½ cup water *or* 1 cup water
1 teaspoon minced garlic
½ teaspoon dried basil leaves
½ teaspoon dried oregano leaves
¼ teaspoon salt
12 ounces lean ground round
12 ounces ground turkey breast
1 cup fresh whole wheat bread crumbs (2 slices whole wheat bread)
½ cup shredded zucchini
¼ cup cholesterol-free egg substitute *or* 2 egg whites

1. Preheat oven to 350°F. Combine tomato paste, wine, water, garlic, basil, oregano and salt in small saucepan. Bring to a boil; reduce heat to low. Simmer, uncovered, 15 minutes. Set aside.

2. Combine remaining ingredients and ½ cup reserved tomato mixture in large bowl. Mix well. Shape into loaf; place into ungreased 9×5×3-inch loaf pan. Bake 45 minutes. Discard any drippings. Pour ½ cup remaining tomato mixture over top of loaf. Bake an additional 15 minutes. Place on serving platter. Cool 10 minutes before slicing. Garnish as desired. **Makes 8 servings**

Nutrients per Serving: 144 Calories (11% of calories from fat), 2g Total Fat, 1g Saturated Fat, 41mg Cholesterol, 171mg Sodium, 19g Protein, 7g Carbohydrate, 1g Dietary Fiber

Italian-Style Meat Loaf

Pepper Steak

1 tablespoon coarsely cracked black pepper
½ teaspoon dried rosemary
2 beef filet mignons or rib-eye steaks, 1 inch thick (4 to 6 ounces each)
1 tablespoon butter or margarine
1 tablespoon vegetable oil
¼ cup brandy or dry red wine

1. Combine pepper and rosemary in bowl. Coat both sides of steaks with mixture.

2. Heat butter and oil in large skillet until hot; add steaks and cook over medium to medium-high heat 5 to 7 minutes per side for medium, or to desired doneness. Remove steaks from skillet. Sprinkle lightly with salt and cover to keep warm.

3. Add brandy to skillet; bring to a boil over high heat, scraping particles from bottom of skillet. Boil about 1 minute or until liquid is reduced by half. Spoon sauce over steaks.

Makes 2 servings

Note: For a special touch, sprinkle chopped parsley over steaks before serving.

Cook's Note: Filet mignon and rib-eye steaks are two of the most tender cuts of meat. These choice cuts are the most expensive and are well-suited to quick, dry-heat cooking methods such as pan-frying, roasting, broiling and grilling.

Prep and Cook Time: 17 minutes

Nutrients per Serving: 392 Calories (55% of calories from fat),
24g Total Fat, 11g Saturated Fat, 84mg Cholesterol, 117mg Sodium,
25g Protein, 2g Carbohydrate, 1g Dietary Fiber

Pepper Steak

Joe's Special

1 pound lean ground beef
2 cups sliced mushrooms
1 small onion, chopped
2 teaspoons Worcestershire sauce
1 teaspoon dried oregano leaves
1 teaspoon ground nutmeg
½ teaspoon garlic powder
½ teaspoon salt
1 package (10 ounces) frozen chopped spinach, thawed
4 large eggs, lightly beaten
⅓ cup grated Parmesan cheese

1. Spray large skillet with nonstick cooking spray. Add ground beef, mushrooms and onion; cook over medium-high heat 6 to 8 minutes or until onion is tender, breaking beef apart with wooden spoon. Add Worcestershire, oregano, nutmeg, garlic powder and salt. Cook until meat is no longer pink.

2. Drain spinach (do not squeeze dry); stir into meat mixture. Push mixture to one side of pan. Reduce heat to medium. Pour eggs into other side of pan; cook, without stirring, 1 to 2 minutes or until set on bottom. Lift eggs to allow uncooked portion to flow underneath. Repeat until softly set. Gently stir into meat mixture and heat through. Stir in cheese.

Makes 4 to 6 servings

Serving Suggestion: Serve with salsa and toast, if desired.

Prep and Cook Time: 20 minutes

Nutrients per Serving: 369 Calories (56% of calories from fat), 23g Total Fat, 11g Saturated Fat, 290mg Cholesterol, 614mg Sodium, 32g Protein, 8g Carbohydrate, 1g Dietary Fiber

Joe's Special

Simmering Fondue

1 pound medium shrimp, peeled
8 ounces beef tenderloin, cut into thin slices
8 ounces lamb loin, cut into thin slices
2 cups sliced mushrooms
2 cups sliced carrots
2 cups broccoli florets
4 cans (about 14 ounces each) reduced-sodium chicken broth
½ cup dry white wine
1 tablespoon chopped fresh parsley
1 teaspoon bottled minced garlic
½ teaspoon dried thyme leaves
½ teaspoon dried rosemary

1. Arrange shrimp, beef, lamb, mushrooms, carrots and broccoli on large serving platter or in individual bowls.

2. Combine chicken broth, wine, parsley, garlic, thyme and rosemary in large saucepan. Bring to a boil over high heat. Remove from heat. Strain broth. Transfer broth to electric wok. Return to a simmer over high heat.

3. Thread any combination shrimp, meat and vegetables onto bamboo skewer or fondue fork. Cook in broth 2 to 3 minutes.

Makes 4 servings

Prep and Cook Time: 20 minutes

Nutrients per Serving: 334 Calories (27% of calories from fat),
10g Total Fat, 2g Saturated Fat, 288mg Cholesterol, 353mg Sodium,
50g Protein, 10g Carbohydrate, 4g Dietary Fiber

Simmering Fondue

Grilled Pork Tenderloin Medallions

Pepper & Herb Rub
  1 tablespoon dried basil leaves
  1 tablespoon garlic salt
  1 tablespoon dried thyme leaves
  1½ teaspoons cracked black pepper
  1½ teaspoons dried rosemary
  1 teaspoon paprika

Pork
  2 tablespoons Pepper & Herb Rub
  12 pork tenderloin medallions (about 1 pound)

1. For rub, combine basil, salt, thyme, pepper, rosemary and paprika in small jar or resealable plastic food storage bag. Store in cool dry place up to 3 months.

2. Prepare barbecue for direct cooking. Sprinkle rub evenly over both sides of pork; pressing lightly. Spray pork with olive-oil-flavored nonstick cooking spray.

3. Place pork on grid over medium-hot coals. Grill, uncovered, 4 to 5 minutes per side or until pork is no longer pink in center.   **Makes 4 servings**

Serving Suggestion: Serve with steamed red potatoes and broccoli, if desired.

Nutrients per Serving: 145 Calories (27% of calories from fat), 4g Total Fat, 1g Saturated Fat, 66mg Cholesterol, 528mg Sodium, 24g Protein, 2g Carbohydrate, 1g Dietary Fiber

Grilled Pork Tenderloin Medallions

August Moon Korean Ribs

⅓ cup water
⅓ cup soy sauce
¼ cup thinly sliced green onions
3 tablespoons dark sesame oil
3 tablespoons honey
2 tablespoons minced garlic
2 tablespoons sesame seeds
1 tablespoon grated fresh ginger
1 teaspoon black pepper
3½ pounds pork back ribs

To prepare marinade, combine all ingredients except ribs in small bowl. Place ribs in large resealable plastic food storage bag. Pour marinade over ribs, turning to coat. Seal bag. Marinate in refrigerator overnight. Arrange medium KINGSFORD® Briquets on each side of rectangular metal or foil drip pan. Grill ribs in center of grid on covered grill 35 to 45 minutes or until ribs are browned and cooked through, turning once.

Makes 8 servings

Nutrients per Serving: 331 Calories (68% of calories from fat), 25g Total Fat, 11g Saturated Fat, 94mg Cholesterol, 111mg Sodium, 23g Protein, 3g Carbohydrate, 1g Dietary Fiber

Steaks with Mushroom Onion Sauce

1½ pounds boneless beef sirloin steak
2 cups sliced fresh mushrooms
1 medium onion, thinly sliced
1 jar (12 ounces) HEINZ® Fat Free Savory Beef Gravy
1 tablespoon HEINZ® Tomato Ketchup
1 teaspoon HEINZ® Worcestershire Sauce
Dash pepper

Cut steak into 6 portions. Spray a large skillet with nonstick cooking spray. Cook steak over medium high heat to desired doneness, about 5 minutes per side for medium-rare. Remove and keep warm. In same skillet, cook mushrooms and onion until liquid evaporates. Stir in gravy, ketchup, Worcestershire sauce and pepper; simmer 1 minute, stirring occasionally. Serve sauce over steak.

Makes 6 servings (about 2 cups sauce)

Nutrients per Serving: 204 Calories (26% of calories from fat), 6g Total Fat, 3g Saturated Fat, 69mg Cholesterol, 127mg Sodium, 27g Protein, 10g Carbohydrate, 1g Dietary Fiber

Peanut Pork Tenderloin

⅓ cup chunky unsweetened peanut butter
⅓ cup regular or light canned coconut milk
¼ cup lemon juice or dry white wine
3 tablespoons soy sauce
3 cloves garlic, minced
2 tablespoons sugar
1 piece (1-inch cube) fresh ginger, minced
½ teaspoon salt
¼ to ½ teaspoon cayenne pepper
¼ teaspoon ground cinnamon
1½ pounds pork tenderloin

Combine peanut butter, coconut milk, lemon juice, soy sauce, garlic, sugar, ginger, salt, cayenne pepper and cinnamon in 2-quart glass dish until blended. Add pork; turn to coat. Cover and refrigerate at least 30 minutes or overnight. Remove pork from marinade; discard marinade. Grill pork on covered grill over medium KINGSFORD® Briquets about 20 minutes until just barely pink in center, turning 4 times. Cut crosswise into ½-inch slices. Serve immediately.   **Makes 4 to 6 servings**

Nutrients per Serving (⅙ of recipe): 429 Calories (50% of calories from fat), 24g Total Fat, 9g Saturated Fat, 106mg Cholesterol, 1230mg Sodium, 40g Protein, 15g Carbohydrate, 2g Dietary Fiber

Grilled Italian Steak

¾ cup WISH-BONE® Italian Dressing*
2 tablespoons grated Parmesan cheese
2 teaspoons dried basil leaves, crushed
¼ teaspoon cracked black pepper
2 to 3-pound boneless sirloin or top round steak

Also terrific with WISH-BONE® Robusto Italian or Lite Italian Dressing.

In large, shallow nonaluminum baking dish or plastic bag, combine all ingredients except steak. Add steak; turn to coat. Cover or close bag and marinate in refrigerator, turning occasionally, 3 to 24 hours.

Remove steak from marinade, reserving marinade. Grill or broil steak, turning once, until steak is done.

Meanwhile, in small saucepan, bring reserved marinade to a boil and continue boiling 1 minute. Pour over steak.   **Makes 8 servings**

Nutrients per Serving: 310 Calories (55% of calories from fat), 19g Total Fat, 3g Saturated Fat, 75mg Cholesterol, 560mg Sodium, 32g Protein, 3g Carbohydrate, <1g Dietary Fiber

London Broil with Marinated Vegetables

¾ cup olive oil
¾ cup red wine
2 tablespoons red wine vinegar
2 tablespoons finely chopped shallots
2 teaspoons bottled minced garlic
½ teaspoon dried marjoram leaves
½ teaspoon dried oregano leaves
½ teaspoon dried basil leaves
½ teaspoon black pepper
2 pounds top round London broil (1½ inches thick)
1 medium red onion, cut into ¼-inch-thick slices
1 package (8 ounces) sliced mushrooms
1 medium red bell pepper, cut into strips
1 medium zucchini, cut into ¼-inch-thick slices

1. Combine olive oil, wine, vinegar, shallots, garlic, marjoram, oregano, basil and pepper in medium bowl; whisk to combine.

2. Combine London broil and ¾ cup marinade in large resealable food storage bag. Seal bag and turn to coat. Marinate up to 24 hours in refrigerator, turning once or twice.

3. Combine onion, mushrooms, bell pepper, zucchini and remaining marinade in separate large food storage bag. Seal bag and turn to coat. Refrigerate up to 24 hours, turning once or twice.

4. Preheat broiler. Remove meat from marinade and place on broiler pan; discard marinade. Broil 4 to 5 inches from heat about 9 minutes per side or until desired doneness. Let stand 10 minutes before slicing. Cut meat into thin slices.

5. While meat is standing, drain marinade from vegetables and arrange on broiler pan. Broil 4 to 5 inches from heat about 9 minutes or until edges of vegetables just begin to brown. Serve meat and vegetables immediately on platter.   **Makes 6 servings**

Make-Ahead Time: up to 1 day before serving
Final Prep and Cook Time: 24 minutes

Nutrients per Serving: 324 Calories (% of calories from fat), 16g Total Fat, 8g Saturated Fat, 75mg Cholesterol, 66mg Sodium, 36g Protein, 8g Carbohydrate, 2g Dietary Fiber

London Broil with Marinated Vegetables

Veal in Gingered Sweet Bell Pepper Sauce

1 teaspoon olive oil
¾ pound veal cutlets, thinly sliced
½ cup skim milk
1 tablespoon finely chopped fresh tarragon
2 teaspoons crushed capers
1 jar (7 ounces) roasted red peppers, drained
1 tablespoon lemon juice
½ teaspoon freshly grated ginger
½ teaspoon black pepper

1. Heat oil in medium saucepan over high heat. Add veal; lightly brown both sides. Reduce heat to medium. Add milk, chopped tarragon and capers. Cook, uncovered, 5 minutes or until veal is fork-tender and milk evaporates.

2. Place roasted peppers, lemon juice, ginger and black pepper in food processor or blender; process until smooth. Set aside.

3. Remove veal from pan with slotted spoon; place in serving dish. Spoon roasted pepper sauce over veal. Sprinkle with cooked capers and fresh tarragon, if desired.

Makes 4 servings

Nutrients per Serving: 120 Calories (31% of calories from fat), 4g Total Fat, 1g Saturated Fat, 54mg Cholesterol, 89mg Sodium, 14g Protein, 6g Carbohydrate, 1g Dietary Fiber

Veal in Gingered Sweet Bell Pepper Sauce

The Definitive Steak

4 New York strip steaks (about 5 ounces each)
4 tablespoons olive oil
2 teaspoons minced garlic
1 teaspoon salt
½ teaspoon black pepper

Place steaks in shallow glass container. Combine oil, garlic, salt and pepper in small bowl; mix well. Pour oil mixture over steaks; turn to coat well. Cover; refrigerate 30 to 60 minutes.

Prepare grill for direct cooking.

Place steaks on grid. Grill, covered, over medium-high heat 14 minutes for medium, 20 minutes for well or to desired doneness, turning halfway through grilling time.

Makes 4 servings

Nutrients per Serving: 347 Calories (60% of calories from fat), 23g Total Fat, 10g Saturated Fat, 66mg Cholesterol, 596mg Sodium, 32g Protein, 1g Carbohydrate, <1g Dietary Fiber

Top to bottom: The Definitive Steak,
Chicken Tikka (page 108)

Delightful

Desserts

Apple Cranberry Mold

    2 cups boiling apple juice
    1 package (8-serving size) *or* **2 packages (4-serving size each) JELL-O® Brand Cranberry Flavor Sugar Free Low Calorie Gelatin,** *or* **any red flavor**
    1½ cups reduced calorie cranberry juice cocktail

STIR boiling juice into gelatin in large bowl at least 2 minutes until completely dissolved. Stir in cranberry juice. Pour into 4-cup mold.

REFRIGERATE 4 hours or until firm. Unmold. Store leftover gelatin mold in refrigerator.

Makes 8 (½-cup) servings

How to Unmold: Dip mold in warm water for about 15 seconds. Gently pull gelatin from around edges with moist fingers. Place moistened serving plate on top of mold. Invert mold and plate; holding mold and plate together, shake slightly to loosen. Gently remove mold and center gelatin on plate.

Prep Time: 10 minutes plus refrigerating

Nutrients per Serving: 45 Calories (0% of calories from fat), 0g Total Fat, 0g Saturated Fat, 0mg Cholesterol, 80mg Sodium, 1g Protein, 10g Carbohydrate, 0g Dietary Fiber

Apple Cranberry Mold

Easy Fruit Tarts

12 wonton skins
  Vegetable cooking spray
  2 tablespoons apple jelly or apricot fruit spread
  1½ cups sliced or cut-up fruit such as DOLE® Bananas, Strawberries or Red or Green Seedless Grapes
  1 cup nonfat or low fat yogurt, any flavor

• Press wonton skins into 12 muffin cups sprayed with vegetable cooking spray, allowing corners to stand up over edges of muffin cups.

• Bake at 375°F 5 minutes or until lightly browned. Carefully remove wonton cups to wire rack; cool.

• Cook and stir jelly in small saucepan over low heat until jelly melts.

• Brush bottoms of cooled wonton cups with melted jelly. Place two fruit slices in each cup; spoon rounded tablespoon of yogurt on top of fruit. Garnish with fruit slice and mint leaves. Serve immediately.   **Makes 12 servings**

Prep Time: 20 minutes
Bake Time: 5 minutes

Nutrients per Serving (1 fruit tart): 57 Calories (5% of calories from fat), <1g Total Fat, <1g Saturated Fat, 2mg Cholesterol, 32mg Sodium, 1g Protein, 12g Carbohydrate, 1g Dietary Fiber

Easy Fruit Tarts

Cherry Almond Supreme

1 can (8 ounces) pitted dark sweet cherries in light syrup, undrained
1 package (4-serving size) JELL-O® Brand Cherry Flavor Sugar Free Gelatin
¾ cup boiling water
    Ice cubes
2 tablespoons chopped toasted almonds
1 cup thawed COOL WHIP® LITE® Whipped Topping

Drain cherries, reserving syrup. If necessary, add enough water to reserved syrup to measure ½ cup. Cut cherries into quarters.

Completely dissolve gelatin in boiling water. Combine measured syrup and enough ice to measure 1¼ cups. Add to gelatin; stir until slightly thickened. Remove any unmelted ice. Chill until thickened. Measure 1¼ cups gelatin; stir in half the cherries and half the nuts. Set aside.

Gently stir whipped topping into remaining gelatin. Add remaining cherries and nuts; spoon into 6 dessert glasses. Chill until set but not firm, about 15 minutes. Top with clear gelatin mixture. Chill until set, about 1 hour.   **Makes 6 servings (about 3 cups)**

Nutrients per Serving: 77 Calories (34% of calories from fat),
3g Total Fat, 1g Saturated Fat, 0mg Cholesterol, 34mg Sodium,
1g Protein, 10g Carbohydrate, 1g Dietary Fiber

Lighter Than Air Chocolate Delight

2 envelopes unflavored gelatin
½ cup cold water
1 cup boiling water
1⅓ cups nonfat dry milk powder
⅓ cup HERSHEY'S Cocoa or HERSHEY'S Dutch Processed Cocoa
1 tablespoon vanilla extract
Dash salt
Granulated sugar substitute to equal 14 teaspoons sugar
8 large ice cubes

1. Sprinkle gelatin over cold water in blender container; let stand 4 minutes to soften. Gently stir with rubber spatula, scraping gelatin particles off sides; add boiling water to gelatin mixture. Cover; blend until gelatin dissolves. Add milk powder, cocoa, vanilla and salt; blend on medium speed until well mixed. Add sugar substitute and ice cubes; blend on high speed until ice is crushed and mixture is smooth and fluffy.

2. Immediately pour mixture into 4-cup mold. Cover; refrigerate until firm. Unmold onto serving plate. **Makes 8 servings**

Note: Eight individual dessert dishes may be used in place of 4-cup mold, if desired.

Nutrients per Serving: 70 Calories (13% of calories from fat),
1g Total Fat, <1g Saturated Fat, 0mg Cholesterol, 105mg Sodium,
6g Protein, 9g Carbohydrate, 1g Dietary Fiber

Low Fat Lemon Soufflé Cheesecake

1 graham cracker, crushed, divided
⅔ cup boiling water
1 package (4-serving size) JELL-O® Brand Lemon Flavor Sugar Free Low
**   Calorie Gelatin Dessert**
1 cup BREAKSTONE'S® or KNUDSEN® 2% Cottage Cheese
1 container (8 ounces) PHILADELPHIA FREE® Fat Free Cream Cheese
2 cups thawed COOL WHIP FREE® Whipped Topping

SPRINKLE ½ of the crumbs onto side of 8- or 9-inch springform pan or 9-inch pie plate which has been sprayed with no stick cooking spray.

STIR boiling water into gelatin in large bowl at least 2 minutes until completely dissolved. Pour into blender container. Add cheeses; cover. Blend on medium speed until smooth, scraping down sides occasionally.

POUR into large bowl. Gently stir in whipped topping. Pour into prepared pan; smooth top. Sprinkle remaining crumbs around outside edge.

REFRIGERATE 4 hours or until set. Remove side of pan just before serving. Store leftover cheesecake in refrigerator.   **Makes 8 servings**

Prep Time: 15 minutes plus refrigerating

Nutrients per Serving: 100 Calories (18% of calories from fat),
2g Total Fat, 1.5g Saturated Fat, 10mg Cholesterol, 300mg Sodium,
9g Protein, 11g Carbohydrate, 0g Dietary Fiber

Low Fat Lemon Soufflé Cheesecake

Fruit Freezies

1½ cups (12 ounces) canned or thawed frozen peach slices, drained
¾ cup peach nectar
1 tablespoon sugar
¼ to ½ teaspoon coconut extract (optional)

1. Place peaches, nectar, sugar and extract in food processor or blender container; process until smooth.

2. Spoon 2 tablespoons fruit mixture into each section of ice cube trays.*

3. Freeze until almost firm. Insert frill pick into each cube; freeze until firm.

Makes 12 servings

Or, pour ⅓ cup fruit mixture into each of 8 plastic pop molds or small paper or plastic cups. Freeze until almost firm. Insert wooden stick into each mold; freeze until firm. Makes 8 servings.

Apricot Freezies: Substitute canned apricot halves for peach slices and apricot nectar for peach nectar.

Pear Freezies: Substitute canned pear slices for peach slices, pear nectar for peach nectar and almond extract for coconut extract.

Pineapple Freezies: Substitute crushed pineapple for peach slices and unsweetened pineapple juice for peach nectar.

Mango Freezies: Substitute chopped fresh mango for canned peach slices and mango nectar for peach nectar. Omit coconut extract.

Nutrients per Serving (2 cubes): 19 Calories (1% of calories from fat), <1g Total Fat, <1g Saturated Fat, 0mg Cholesterol, 2mg Sodium, <1g Protein, 5g Carbohydrate, <1g Dietary Fiber

Fruit Freezies

Applesauce Yogurt Delight

1 cup boiling water
1 package (4-serving size) JELL-O® Brand Sugar Free Low Calorie Gelatin, any red flavor
¾ cup chilled applesauce
¼ teaspoon ground cinnamon
½ cup BREYERS® Vanilla Lowfat Yogurt

STIR boiling water into gelatin in medium bowl at least 2 minutes until completely dissolved. Measure ¾ cup; stir in applesauce and cinnamon. Pour into bowl or 4 dessert dishes. Refrigerate until set but not firm.

REFRIGERATE remaining gelatin until slightly thickened (consistency of unbeaten egg whites). Mix in yogurt; spoon over gelatin in bowl.

REFRIGERATE 2 hours or until set.   **Makes 4 servings**

Prep Time: 15 minutes plus refrigerating

Nutrients per Serving: 60 Calories (0% of calories from fat), 0g Total Fat, 0g Saturated Fat, <5mg Cholesterol, 90mg Sodium, 3g Protein, 10g Carbohydrate, <1g Dietary Fiber

Apricot and Toasted Almond Phyllo Cups

½ cup low-fat (1%) cottage cheese
4 ounces reduced-fat cream cheese
2 packets sugar substitute *or* equivalent of 4 teaspoons sugar
1 tablespoon fat-free (skim) milk
¼ teaspoon vanilla
4 sheets phyllo dough
  Butter-flavored nonstick cooking spray
3 tablespoons apricot or blackberry preserves
¼ cup sliced almonds, toasted

1. Preheat oven 350°F. Coat 8 (2½-inch) muffin cups with nonstick cooking spray; set aside.

2. Beat cottage cheese, cream cheese, sugar substitute, milk and vanilla in large bowl with electric mixer at high speed until completely smooth; refrigerate until needed.

3. Place 1 sheet phyllo dough on work surface. Keep remaining sheets covered with plastic wrap and damp kitchen towel. Lightly spray phyllo sheet with nonstick cooking spray; top with another sheet; spray with nonstick cooking spray. Repeat with remaining sheets of phyllo.

4. Cut stack of phyllo into 8 pieces using sharp knife or kitchen scissors. Gently fit each stacked square into prepared muffin cup. Bake 5 minutes or until lightly browned; cool on wire rack.

5. Place preserves in small microwavable bowl. Microwave at HIGH 20 seconds or until just melted. Spoon 2 tablespoons cream cheese mixture into each phyllo cup; drizzle 1 teaspoon melted preserves on top of cheese mixture. Top with 1½ teaspoons almonds.   **Makes 8 servings**

Nutrients per Serving: 109 Calories (41% of calories from fat), 5g Total Fat, 2g Saturated Fat, 8mg Cholesterol, 174mg Sodium, 5g Protein, 12g Carbohydrate, 1g Dietary Fiber

Florida Sunshine Cups

¾ cup boiling water
1 package (4-serving size) JELL-O® Brand Orange or Lemon Flavor Sugar Free
    Low Calorie Gelatin
1 cup cold orange juice
½ cup fresh raspberries
1 can (11 ounces) mandarin orange segments, drained

STIR boiling water into gelatin in large bowl at least 2 minutes until completely dissolved. Stir in cold juice. Refrigerate 1½ hours or until thickened (spoon drawn through leaves definite impression).

MEASURE ¾ cup thickened gelatin into medium bowl; set aside. Stir fruit into remaining gelatin. Pour into serving bowl or 6 dessert dishes.

BEAT reserved gelatin with electric mixer on high speed until fluffy and about doubled in volume. Spoon over gelatin in bowl or dishes.

REFRIGERATE 3 hours or until firm.   **Makes 6 servings**

Prep Time: 20 minutes
Refrigerate Time: 4½ hours

Nutrients per Serving (1 sunshine cup): 50 Calories (3% of calories from fat), <1g Total Fat, <1g Saturated Fat, 0mg Cholesterol, 46mg Sodium, 1g Protein, 10g Carbohydrate, 1g Dietary Fiber

Florida Sunshine Cups

Cinnamon Flats

1¾ cups all-purpose flour
½ cup sugar
1½ teaspoons ground cinnamon
¼ teaspoon ground nutmeg
¼ teaspoon salt
8 tablespoons cold margarine
3 egg whites, divided
1 teaspoon vanilla
1 teaspoon water
Sugar Glaze (recipe follows)

1. Preheat oven to 350°F. Combine flour, sugar, 1½ teaspoons cinnamon, nutmeg and salt in medium bowl. Cut in margarine with pastry blender or two knives until mixture forms coarse crumbs. Beat in 2 egg whites and vanilla, forming crumbly mixture; mix with hands to form soft dough.

2. Divide dough into 6 equal pieces and place, evenly spaced, on greased 15×10-inch jelly-roll pan. Spread dough evenly to edges of pan using hands; smooth top of dough with metal spatula or palms of hands. Mix remaining egg white and water in small cup; brush over top of dough. Lightly score dough into 2×1½-inch squares.

3. Bake 20 to 25 minutes or until lightly browned and firm when lightly touched with fingertip. While still warm, cut into squares; drizzle or spread Sugar Glaze over squares. Let stand 15 minutes or until glaze is firm before removing from pan.

Makes 50 cookies

Sugar Glaze

1½ cups powdered sugar
2 to 3 tablespoons skim milk
1 teaspoon vanilla

Combine powdered sugar, 2 tablespoons milk and vanilla in small bowl. If glaze is too thick, add remaining 1 tablespoon milk.   **Makes about ¾ cup**

Nutrients per Serving: 48 Calories (18% of calories from fat),
1g Total Fat, trace Saturated Fat, <1mg Cholesterol, 35mg Sodium,
1g Protein, 9g Carbohydrate, <1g Dietary Fiber

Cinnamon Flats

Chocolate-Peanut Butter-Apple Treats

½ (8-ounce package) fat-free or reduced-fat cream cheese, softened
¼ cup reduced-fat chunky peanut butter
2 tablespoons mini chocolate chips
2 large apples

1. Combine cream cheese, peanut butter and chocolate chips in a small bowl; mix well.

2. Cut each apple into 12 wedges; discard stems and seeds. Spread about 1½ teaspoons of the mixture over each apple slice.

Makes 8 servings (4 apple wedges and 1½ teaspoons spread)

Nutrients per Serving: 101 Calories (37% of calories from fat),
4g Total Fat, 1g Saturated Fat, 2mg Cholesterol, 144mg Sodium,
4g Protein, 12g Carbohydrate, 2g Dietary Fiber

Cranberry-Orange Bread Pudding

2 cups cubed cinnamon bread
¼ cup dried cranberries
2 cups low-fat (1%) milk
1 package (4 serving size) sugar-free vanilla pudding and pie filling mix*
½ cup cholesterol-free egg substitute
1 teaspoon vanilla
1 teaspoon grated orange peel
½ teaspoon ground cinnamon
Low-fat no-sugar-added vanilla ice cream (optional)

*Do not use instant pudding and pie filling.

1. Preheat oven to 325°F. Spray 9 custard cups with nonstick cooking spray.

2. Place bread cubes in custard cups. Bake 10 minutes; add cranberries.

3. Combine remaining ingredients except ice cream in medium bowl. Carefully pour over mixture in custard cups. Let stand 5 to 10 minutes.

4. Place cups on baking sheet; bake 25 to 30 minutes or until center is almost set. Let stand 10 minutes. Serve with ice cream if desired. **Makes 9 servings**

Nutrients per Serving: 67 Calories (13% of calories from fat),
1g Total Fat, <1g Saturated Fat, 2mg Cholesterol, 190mg Sodium,
4g Protein, 11g Carbohydrate, <1g Dietary Fiber

Baked Vanilla Custard

1 quart skim milk
6 eggs
6¼ teaspoons EQUAL® FOR RECIPES *or* 21 packets EQUAL® sweetener *or* ¾ cup
plus 2 tablespoons EQUAL® SPOONFUL™
2 teaspoons vanilla
¼ teaspoon salt
Ground nutmeg

• Heat milk just to boiling in medium saucepan; let cool 5 minutes.

• Beat eggs, Equal®, vanilla and salt in large bowl until smooth; gradually beat in hot milk. Pour mixture into 10 custard cups or 1½-quart glass casserole; sprinkle generously with nutmeg. Place custard cups or casserole in roasting pan; add 1 inch hot water to roasting pan.

• Bake, uncovered, in preheated 325°F oven until sharp knife inserted halfway between center and edge of custard comes out clean, 45 to 60 minutes. Remove custard dishes from roasting pan; cool on wire rack. Refrigerate until chilled.

Makes 10 (½-cup) servings

Nutrients per Serving: 90 Calories (30% of calories from fat),
3g Total Fat, 1g Saturated Fat, 129mg Cholesterol, 142mg Sodium,
7g Protein, 8g Carbohydrate, 0g Dietary Fiber

Peach Melba Dessert

1½ cups boiling water, divided
  2 packages (4-serving size) JELL-O® Brand Raspberry Flavor Sugar Free Low
    Calorie Gelatin Dessert or JELL-O® Brand Raspberry Flavor Gelatin
    Dessert, divided
  1 container (8 ounces) BREYERS® Vanilla Lowfat Yogurt
  1 cup raspberries, divided
  1 can (8 ounces) peach slices in juice, undrained
    Cold water

STIR ¾ cup boiling water into 1 package of gelatin in large bowl at least 2 minutes or until completely dissolved. Refrigerate about 1 hour or until slightly thickened (consistency of unbeaten egg whites). Stir in yogurt and ½ cup raspberries. Reserve remaining raspberries for garnish. Pour gelatin mixture into serving bowl. Refrigerate about 2 hours or until set but not firm (gelatin should stick to finger when touched and should mound).

MEANWHILE, drain peaches, reserving juice. Add cold water to reserved juice to make 1 cup; set aside. Stir remaining ¾ cup boiling water into remaining package gelatin in large bowl at least 2 minutes until completely dissolved. Stir in measured juice and water. Refrigerate about 1 hour or until slightly thickened (consistency of unbeaten egg whites).

RESERVE several peach slices for garnish; chop remaining peaches. Stir chopped peaches into slightly thickened gelatin. Spoon over gelatin layer in bowl. Refrigerate 3 hours or until firm. Top with reserved peach slices and raspberries.

Makes 8 servings

Preparation Time: 20 minutes
Refrigerating Time: 6 hours

Nutrients per Serving (⅛ of total recipe, using JELL-O® Brand Raspberry Flavor Sugar Free Low Calorie Gelatin Dessert): 64 Calories (9% of calories from fat), 1g Total Fat, <1g Saturated Fat, 2mg Cholesterol, 81mg Sodium, 3g Protein, 11g Carbohydrate, 1g Dietary Fiber

Peach Melba Dessert

Conversation Heart Cereal Treats

2 tablespoons margarine or butter
20 large marshmallows
 3 cups frosted oat cereal with marshmallow bits
12 large conversation hearts

1. Line 8- or 9-inch square pan with aluminum foil, leaving 2-inch overhangs on 2 sides. Generously grease or spray with nonstick cooking spray.

2. Melt margarine and marshmallows in medium saucepan over medium heat 3 minutes or until melted and smooth, stirring constantly. Remove from heat.

3. Add cereal; stir until completely coated. Spread in prepared pan; press evenly onto bottom using greased rubber spatula. Press heart candies into top of treats while still warm, evenly spacing to allow 1 heart per bar. Let cool 10 minutes. Using foil overhangs as handles, remove treats from pan. Cut into 12 bars.   **Makes 12 bars**

Prep and Cook Time: 18 minutes

Nutrients per Serving: 62 Calories (29% of calories from fat), 2g Total Fat, 1g Saturated Fat, 0mg Cholesterol, 62mg Sodium, 1g Protein, 11g Carbohydrate, <1g Dietary Fiber

Conversation Heart Cereal Treats

White Sangria Splash

1 cup dry white wine
1 package (8-serving size) *or* 2 packages (4-serving size) JELL-O® Brand
    Lemon Flavor Sugar Free Low Calorie Gelatin Dessert or JELL-O® Brand
    Lemon Flavor Gelatin Dessert
3 cups cold seltzer or club soda
1 tablespoon lime juice
1 tablespoon orange juice or orange liqueur
3 cups seedless grapes, divided
1 cup sliced strawberries
1 cup whole small strawberries

BRING wine to boil in small saucepan. Stir boiling wine into gelatin in medium bowl at least 2 minutes until completely dissolved. Stir in cold seltzer and lime and orange juices. Place bowl of gelatin in larger bowl of ice and water. Let stand about 10 minutes or until thickened (spoon drawn through leaves definite impression), stirring occasionally.

STIR in 1 cup of the grapes and the sliced strawberries. Pour into 6-cup mold.

REFRIGERATE 4 hours or until firm. Unmold. Garnish with remaining grapes and whole strawberries.   **Makes 12 servings**

Preparation Time: 15 minutes
Refrigerating Time: 4 hours

Nutrients per Serving (using JELL-O® Brand Lemon Flavor Sugar Free Low Calorie Gelatin Dessert and orange juice): 60 Calories (0% of calories from fat), 0g Total Fat, 0g Saturated Fat, 0mg Cholesterol, 55mg Sodium, 1g Protein, 9g Carbohydrate, 1g Dietary Fiber

Pears with Strawberry Sweet Dipping Cream

4 ounces fresh or frozen, thawed unsweetened strawberries
¼ cup reduced-fat spreadable cream cheese
¼ cup nonfat plain yogurt
2 packets sugar substitute
½ teaspoon vanilla
2 medium pears, cut in ½-inch slices

1. Process strawberries in blender or food processor until coarsely chopped. Add cream cheese, yogurt, sugar substitute and vanilla. Cover and process until smooth.

2. To serve, dip pear slices in cream cheese mixture.   **Makes 8 servings**

Nutrients per Serving: 52 Calories (25% of calories from fat),
1g Total Fat, 1g Saturated Fat, 4mg Cholesterol, 43mg Sodium,
2g Protein, 8g Carbohydrate, 1g Dietary Fiber

Quick Chocolate Pudding

¼ cup unsweetened cocoa powder
2 tablespoons cornstarch
1½ cups reduced-fat (2%) milk
6 to 8 packets sugar substitute or equivalent of ⅓ cup sugar
1 teaspoon vanilla
⅛ teaspoon ground cinnamon (optional)
Assorted sugar-free candies (optional)

1. Combine cocoa powder and cornstarch in medium microwavable bowl or 1-quart glass measure. Gradually whisk in milk until well blended.

2. Microwave at HIGH 2 minutes; stir. Microwave at MEDIUM-HIGH (70% power) 3 to 4½ minutes or until thickened, stirring every 1½ minutes.

3. Stir in sugar substitute, vanilla and cinnamon, if desired. Let stand at least 5 minutes before serving, stirring occasionally to prevent skin from forming. Serve warm or chilled. Garnish with candies just before serving, if desired.

Makes 4 servings

Nutrients per Serving: 78 Calories (21% of calories from fat),
2g Total Fat, 1g Saturated Fat, 7mg Cholesterol, 56mg Sodium,
5g Protein, 10g Carbohydrate, <1g Dietary Fiber

Yogurt Fluff

¾ cup boiling water
1 package (4-serving size) JELL-O® Brand Sugar Free Low Calorie Gelatin
   Dessert or JELL-O® Brand Gelatin Dessert, any flavor
½ cup cold water or fruit juice
   Ice cubes
1 container (8 ounces) BREYERS® Vanilla Lowfat Yogurt
½ teaspoon vanilla (optional)
5 tablespoons thawed COOL WHIP FREE® or COOL WHIP LITE® Whipped
   Topping

STIR boiling water into gelatin in large bowl at least 2 minutes until completely dissolved.

MIX cold water and ice cubes to make 1 cup. Add to gelatin, stirring until slightly thickened. Remove any remaining ice. Stir in yogurt and vanilla. Pour into dessert dishes.

REFRIGERATE 1½ hours or until firm. Top with whipped topping.

Makes 5 servings

Preparation Time: 10 minutes
Refrigerating Time: 1½ hours

Nutrients per Serving (⅕ of total recipe, using JELL-O® Brand Sugar
Free Low Calorie Gelatin Dessert, water and COOL WHIP FREE®):
61 Calories (13% of calories from fat), 1g Total Fat, <1g Saturated Fat,
3mg Cholesterol, 92mg Sodium, 3g Protein, 9g Carbohydrate,
0g Dietary Fiber

Yogurt Fluff

Strawberry Lime Dessert

2 cups boiling water, divided
1 package (4-serving size) JELL-O® Brand Lime Flavor Sugar Free Low Calorie Gelatin Dessert or JELL-O® Brand Lime Flavor Gelatin Dessert
½ cup cold water
1 container (8 ounces) BREYERS® Vanilla Lowfat Yogurt
1 package (4-serving size) JELL-O® Brand Strawberry Flavor Sugar Free Low Calorie Gelatin Dessert or JELL-O® Brand Strawberry Flavor Gelatin Dessert
1 package (10 ounces) frozen strawberries in lite syrup, unthawed

STIR 1 cup of boiling water into lime gelatin in medium bowl at least 2 minutes until completely dissolved. Stir in cold water. Refrigerate about 45 minutes or until slightly thickened (consistency of unbeaten egg whites). Stir in yogurt with wire whisk until smooth. Pour into 2-quart serving bowl. Refrigerate about 15 minutes or until set but not firm (gelatin should stick to finger when touched and should mound).

STIR remaining 1 cup boiling water into strawberry gelatin in medium bowl at least 2 minutes until completely dissolved. Stir in frozen berries until berries are separated and gelatin is thickened (spoon drawn through leaves definite impression). Spoon over lime gelatin mixture.

REFRIGERATE 2 hours or until firm. Garnish as desired.   **Makes 10 servings**

Preparation Time: 15 minutes
Refrigerating Time: 3 hours

Nutrients per Serving (using JELL-O® Brand Strawberry and Lime Flavors Sugar Free Low Calorie Gelatin Dessert and omitting garnish):
60 Calories (0% of calories from fat), 0g Total Fat, 0g Saturated Fat, <5mg Cholesterol, 65mg Sodium, 2g Protein, 11g Carbohydrate, <1g Dietary Fiber

Strawberry Lime Dessert

Peach Custard

½ cup peeled fresh peach or nectarine cut into chunks
1 can (5 ounces) evaporated skimmed milk*
¼ cup cholesterol-free egg substitute
1 packet sugar substitute *or* equivalent of 2 teaspoons sugar
½ teaspoon vanilla
   Cinnamon

If a 5-ounce can is not available, use ½ cup plus 2 tablespoons evaporated skimmed milk.

1. Preheat oven to 325°F. Divide peach chunks between two 6-ounce ovenproof custard cups. Whisk together milk, egg substitute, sugar substitute and vanilla. Pour mixture over peach chunks in custard cups.

2. Place custard cups in shallow 1-quart casserole. Carefully pour hot water into casserole to depth of 1-inch. Bake custards 50 minutes or until knife inserted in center comes out clean. Remove custard cups from water bath. Serve warm or at room temperature; sprinkle with cinnamon. **Makes 2 servings**

Note: Drained canned peach slices in juice may be substituted for fresh fruit.

Nutrients per Serving: 52 Calories (2% of calories from fat), <1g Total Fat, <1g Saturated Fat, <1mg Cholesterol, 71mg Sodium, 5g Protein, 7g Carbohydrate, 1g Dietary Fiber

Jell-O® Juicy Jigglers®

2½ cups boiling juice (Do not add cold water.)
1 package (8-serving size) *or* **2 packages (4-serving size each) JELL-O® Brand Strawberry Flavor Gelatin or JELL-O Brand Gelatin, any flavor**
1 package (8-serving size) *or* **2 packages (4-serving size each) JELL-O® Brand Strawberry Flavor Sugar Free Low Calorie Gelatin or JELL-O Brand Sugar Free Low Calorie Gelatin, any flavor**

STIR boiling juice into gelatins in large bowl at least 3 minutes until completely dissolved. Pour into 13×9-inch pan.

REFRIGERATE at least 3 hours or until firm (does not stick to finger when touched).

DIP bottom of pan in warm water about 15 seconds. Cut into decorative shapes with cookie cutters all the way through gelatin or cut into 1-inch squares. Lift from pan.

Makes about 24 pieces

Prep: 10 minutes plus refrigerating

> **Nutrients per Serving:** 40 Calories (0% of calories from fat),
> 0g Total Fat, 0g Saturated Fat, 0mg Cholesterol, 50mg Sodium,
> 1g Protein, 9g Carbohydrate, 0g Dietary Fiber

Bread Pudding Snacks

1¼ cups reduced-fat (2%) milk
½ cup cholesterol-free egg substitute
⅓ cup sugar
1 teaspoon vanilla
⅛ teaspoon salt
⅛ teaspoon ground nutmeg (optional)
4 cups (½-inch) cinnamon or cinnamon-raisin bread cubes (about 6 bread slices)
1 tablespoon margarine or butter, melted

1. Combine milk, egg substitute, sugar, vanilla, salt and nutmeg in medium bowl; mix well. Add bread; mix until well moistened. Let stand at room temperature 15 minutes.

2. Preheat oven to 350°F. Line 12 medium-sized muffin cups with paper liners.

3. Spoon bread mixture evenly into prepared cups; drizzle evenly with margarine.

4. Bake 30 to 35 minutes or until snacks are puffed and golden brown. Remove to wire rack to cool completely.   **Makes 12 servings**

Note: Snacks will puff up in the oven and fall slightly upon cooling.

Nutrients per Serving: 72 Calories (22% of calories from fat), 2g Total Fat, 1g Saturated Fat, 2mg Cholesterol, 93mg Sodium, 2g Protein, 12g Carbohydrate, 0g Dietary Fiber